The Ethereal Hike

Printed in the United States of America

First Printing, 2019

ISBN 978-0-578-56382-4

Foreword

The *Ethereal Hike* is a journey into the deepest depths of the soul of a mother who has been through what seems to be every parent's worst nightmare — losing a child. The pain and the love that comes along with going through her trials and tribulations illuminates through the words on the pages. It is a tragic and triumphant love story that sheds light on how one can be severely crushed and become intensely aligned with the Supreme Being. Adjua Styles offers courage and strength as she takes readers behind the scenes of young motherhood with a lack of elderly guidance and gorging stability amid trauma; rooting her family in all of life's shifts. Growing up in Brooklyn, New York in addition to the loss of a child, has made her who she is — nothing less than amazing to read, to say the least.

This book is a human tornado of emotions that is bound to sweep you off your feet and cause you to think about who you are and what you are made of. I truly believe that this book is a testament that the Creator possibly crushes people who he chooses to be the anointed because the words in this book have shed a light on me that can never be taken away, not even on the darkest nights.

Mr. Styles aka Styles P The Ghost

To Tai, my little butterfly, whose light will eternally reflect through my soul.

Table of Contents

PART I

INTRODUCTION

Choosing to Thrive

I never considered myself worthy enough to wear the hat of *survivor* until I acknowledged my traumatic birthing blueprint and my daughter's passing. I was forced to process this correlation after such a sudden loss. From conception, angst, pressure, and pain would become my first companions in life. I was initially *branded* by these hindrances and emotions, however, thankfully they became the catalysts for receiving extra strength. This strength is the foundation of my survival and growth obtained from the privilege of loss. In this life, we all experience certain loss and trauma that does not have to define who we are in the world. A marriage to trauma and pain should not be life goals. Being pardoned by God serving as a mother to my daughter in the physical has given me such purpose and insight. But this insight came after many external hardships and internal growth. This story, my story, is meant to help you look at your life as well and harness the growth, purpose, and insight we all possess. This process has revealed a strength that I didn't know I personally possessed. It's an intuitive and spiritual strength that is guided by an intense light force — spearheaded by my daughter.

The first step to healing this soulful loss was to be willing to explore my childhood and early traumas. This process was necessary in order to understand the root cause of my triggers, my problems, and my pain.

The person I was previously no longer exists. It is said that losing a child is the worst thing that can happen to any parent. I must agree. For me, it was as if I lived with an expansive emotional noose of grief, guilt, anxiety, and loss that fluctuated daily. The pain that the loss of a child brings is so aching, traumatizing, and debilitating, yet simultaneously awakening. In turn, this evolution must be shared. It is a pain that has biologically and psychologically transformed me.

However, it has transformed me with a kind of resilience, love of self, and a keen connection to the universe. This revision has brought forth the best version of me that I never had or ever known. In this, I hope you follow along with me to unearth the best version of yourself.

When starting this journey, *to be judged or not to be judged* was the monotonous chant pacing like a raging bull inside my head. Back slated against the birch wood-paneled headboard, knees clutched tight to my chest, I sat in my traditional thinking pose. My chin wedged in my knees; tears streamed down my arms and shins. I was in a state of panic, but still coherent. And, I sat there. Sitting in that stillness lasted for weeks until my soul crept in gently and submissively saying, "You need to be released from you! You are strong, but you are human first.

Why suppress anything after what you've just been through? Honor your daughter. Honor yourself!"

I am the only one who knows my life story and the emotional torment endured every single day that passed. I've lived in doubt, straddling the fence unsteadily every single day, which is not only tiring but also a form of self-captivity. I had every muscle clenched tightly and was holding on to the same space; trying not to fall over in fear of making a choice. The overthinking was putting a mental constraint on me and it was prohibiting my growth. I would often say, "I cannot live or love myself adequately as a GMO caged bird."

I didn't want the traumatic experiences I've lived through to stunt my growth. I'd tell God, "I still want to grow. I still want to love. I don't want my light to go out." I finally stopped grappling with my heart and mind's reluctance, regarding releasing my story. I dropped all of my expectations, owned my fears, and grabbed my God-given freedom. I reclaimed my peace of mind! I needed a complete mind, body, and spiritual alignment in order to proceed forward. In turn, this would allow me to be a healthy wife and mother to my son. In order to maintain a strong healing flow, I needed a cathartic purge but one that would serve others as well. I've taken pride in being honest and deliberately raw, but still tender in sharing these memoirs. If word of mouth leads you here, it just means that God has answered my prayers. If kinship leads you here, then, Godspeed!

The truth is that when you have the notion of turning lemons into lemonade, you don't have a clue who will be open to drink your wisdom and lessons learned. You are just ready to serve. This book is my strength and my survival served on a platter.

The inadvertent discipline, self-awareness, and overall strength that you *now* see are just the cherries on top. I see this gift of strength as an asset; essential to why I'm standing here today. My husband is also critical to why I'm standing here today, as is my son and my daughter's spirit. I'm a survivor. We, my family, are survivors. If you're living in hardship and perseverance, you are absolutely a survivor.

How can your strength be mimicked, imprinted, or even perceived, if there's no genuine transparency? *The Ethereal Hike* is mine. Respecting myself and loving myself *hard* has grown into a sport. I'm an overachiever with an abundance of self-love.

While everything may seem peachy now, I needed serious restoration before attempting any act of love, let alone self-love. How was I to love my children properly if I couldn't love myself? How could I maintain a healthy marriage if I didn't love myself? Just because someone has children and/or is married, doesn't mean that they know how to love. I believe that God's plan for my life was to face many challenges with all routes ultimately leading to Him.

I'm not perfect and I will never own that title. I have not attained the state of enlightenment— yet. But, perhaps, I could assist by remedying those uncomfortable, irritating thoughts that are taking shuttles back and forth in your brain. This book is for anyone who feels like no one understands or is willing to comprehend them without judgement. For anyone who is afraid to simply say that they have thought of dying or taking a break from their reality. "It's okay...you are human.

There is a simple reason why I am writing my story. I am not writing for the money or fame. I am not writing this to directly focus on the loss of my daughter. I am writing because I believe my story can help others love themselves more. I can help you be kindhearted to yourself and have more patience. Using my personal experiences, I can help you survive, which only makes for a better world. Take into consideration that despite your traumatic wardrobe, you can show your best self every single day, without pity, perhaps in clothing straight off the runway. That is truly living and thriving. Honor it.

Take advantage of my awareness and the opportunity to look through my personal lens — with the intention that you see yourself, a friend, or a family member as a human being, not a superhero. I'm praying that you walk away having been seen.

CHAPTER 1

A Knock at the Door

Thursday, June 25, 2015. I woke up pretty early, before 8:00 am, missing the usual warmth that came from my husband's side of the bed. When he's away I struggle to keep my eyes closed for the night and certainly into the morning too. I'm surprised I'd slept at all; suffering from my own brand of separation anxiety. My morning routine consisted of calling hubby immediately upon waking up and before moving out of bed. From there, I made my daily organic smoothie consisting of kale, chard, frozen strawberries, vegetable protein powder, a squeeze of lemon, chia seeds, and diluted apple juice. Then, I prepared to walk Madonna, my beautiful black Patterdale Terrier that my husband bought some time ago while I was away in Florida. I must admit that I was a bit jealous of her, at first, because of their connection and her ignorance toward me. I knew that we would get close once she got a real dose of my energy.

She has provided comfort that humans just cannot supply. The healing and love that Madonna offers is so unusual yet so satisfying. What isn't satisfying is her waiting at the foot of my bed, staring like a maniac to go for a walk — as she did this very moment. The walk would be a mixture of things — some exercise for me, some exercise for her, and detective work; one of my favorite things to do while I get fresh air. I'll be honest and say that a rapper's girlfriend makes the best detective; I've been trained.

Nonetheless, I made my way outside. I was familiar with the area, just not the street I lived on. Madonna and I went on a journey down this new street together in search of anything, honestly. I was still getting familiar with faces, dogs, and homes in this new move for our family. I made a right out of our complex and adjacent to us stood another complex. It was an older styled area with residents who seemed to have lived there for decades. Their eyes were glued to the new Styles in the neighborhood and when walking Madonna, the stares of seniority were peppered within every block. I began to walk on the communal lawn and the glances transformed into bulging eyes, which grew more intense the further I walked down the street. While minding my business, I proceeded to keep walking my dog, sh*t bag in tow and tried not to make any more eye contact. I didn't want there to be any altercations. It was too early and Westchester cops and black people just don't mix. As I slowly began to move and walk in one direction, a tall slender man charged after me yelling and screaming. He yelled at the top of his lungs, telling me to get off the lawn.

I couldn't quite make out what he said but he proceeded to scream something about *black*. I told him to politely shut up and not to approach me as he had. I don't know what the something black meant or what he was referring to. Honestly, he could have been talking about the dog, but I had no clue and I didn't like his tone or body language. I walked off and called the police. I wanted documentation of racial slurs before any further drama transpired. The police came over, prepared a report, and it was done. However, I didn't appreciate the negative energy so early in the morning.

As soon as I entered my home, I received a text from my daughter, Tai. It was around 10:20 AM, "I'm tired of my girlfriend's shit. We're breaking up and I want to come home."

She was contacting me from her girlfriend's phone. The next message came through, "I'm leaving the house. Don't respond on here, but I will call you."

I had received similar text messages before, so I wasn't too alarmed. I was more confused at the "don't respond," because now I had to wait. But, I did.

As the mother of a young adult, I have learned the hard way to respect my daughter's wishes. Plus, my mom was still in Florida where Tai now lived. My mother was retired and seemingly always available. I wouldn't wait too long but I wanted to give Tai some time and was afraid of treating her like an infant too soon. The text messages didn't sit well with me, especially after my negative exchange with the slender man just minutes ago. My antennae were up as Madonna paced her way around the kitchen floor. "It's too early for people to be so miserable," I said to myself. I left the text alone for the moment believing Tai just needed a little time. I escaped to the hair salon - a place of refuge for many women I knew. My husband and I were leaving the next day for Los Angeles. Therefore, a hair and a lunch date with a friend in the city were on the books. However, throughout the next few hours my antennae never retreated.

After some time had passed, I reached out to Tai and received no response. Having a young adult daughter means balancing their independence with your motherly instincts. I then reached out to her girlfriend's phone and still received no answer. I wasn't too worried just yet. I wrapped up what I was doing downtown and proceeded to head home.

Once finally inside, I tried to calm my mind and immediately began to peel the potatoes for my infamous vegan potato salad. I cut up the potatoes, threw them in the boiling pot and went upstairs to wrap up my hair to avoid the steam, food scents, and the grease from latching on. I changed from my outside clothes to pajama pants and a tee, then went back down to the kitchen to really get my hands dirty. Hubby was en route home so I wanted to ensure that a hot meal awaited him. It was Thursday, a school day. Therefore, I knew that my son Noah would come through the door at any moment — only to drop his things off, kiss me, and double back out the door. I was messing around in the kitchen, trying to figure out what else I'd cook when it dawned on me that I hadn't heard back from Tai. I started to worry slightly and proceeded to text her multiple times. "Where is she?!" I said aloud to no one. Tai is the type of person who won't hesitate to call and ask for assistance if she needs help or is in trouble. So, I didn't take my worry to the deep end, treading lightly among frustration.

"Hi, Ma!" It was Noah, bursting through the door. He's my little saint, smiling with his perfect teeth, greeting me happily, as always. It was a two-second privilege that he gave before bolting straight to his room. Computers, video games, dirt bikes, and girls ran his world. Only Noah knew what was on his extracurricular to-do list. Unfortunately, I had to interrupt his after-school planning so that I could harass him to walk Madonna as I continued cooking.

One hour later, with a meal almost complete, a few knocks on the door pulled me from the kitchen. I walked to the front of the house wondering, who could this be? I looked through the peephole and a police uniform looked back at me. There were two men — one outfitted as an officer and the other in a plain white shirt. I couldn't make out if the man in the white shirt was a cop or not.

"Who is it?" I said as if I couldn't see who stood beyond the door. I needed verbal confirmation. They replied, almost in unison, "White Plains Police Department." Luckily, I hadn't just hit a joint. Finally, ready to comply, I reached to open the door. Just before I turned the lock, I thought to abruptly ask, "May I help you?" I'm no criminal and I didn't have any cases. Therefore, I didn't do anything — not to mention that my husband wasn't home.

One of the officers said, "We need to come in and speak to Mrs. Styles." I peculiarly replied, "How do you know my name?"

The officers and I went back and forth a bit because I wanted clarification for their visit prior to opening the door. I was intrigued. Though, I gave in and finally allowed them to come in.

"Does this have anything to do with my neighbors from earlier?" I immediately asked. They said no.

I apologized for being a bit hasty and during my apology, I realized that the other man who was wearing the white shirt was in fact a cop — he looked like the head of the department, someone who only handles serious situations. He turned to me and asked, "Are you Tai Hing's mother?"

"Yes." I replied.

CHAPTER 2

A Rocky Foundation, A Family Upending

July, 1991.

For as long as I can remember, my mother has been on some journey with ankhs, ohms, and crystals in tow. Her spiritual voyage has remained evidently consistent to me. In my eyes, this was a crucial block in the unstable foundation that was my own childhood. As an adult, knowing and realizing that my mother had always been on the search for something is vital to my understanding of her, myself, and my lineage. My mother was searching for something so much that I felt neglected at times. It was almost as if her search or need for the companionship of others was greater than the need for her children. A hard reality for a child to accept. I was devastated as a kid when I had to leave her and move with my dad. I was leaving a crucial block of my foundation, love, and trust in the version of a mother.

"Uticaaaa! Uticaaaa!" shouted the West Indian men that were advertising their businesses. It was the aggressive West

Indian way of saying Utica Ave. Old folks, children, and even stray dogs, at some point, have all been startled and irritated by their presence. The men had a loud approach like the Crazy Eddie commercials of the '80s. They meant well. However, they were clearly ignorant to how harsh their attitudes were. In the '90s, various men offered a certain service for locals who need-ed alternative modes of transportation. It was called Dollar Van Service. The name quite indicative of the service, just one dol-lar for a ride given by a complete stranger. The drivers solicit 24 hours, 7 days a week, on a main strip in certain areas. It was a really smart, illegal business, but also very convenient and ac-commodating for people living in two fare zones — like I did. The hustle was indicative of the resilient people who lived there — the products of Brooklyn — the gritty yet pretty, rough and tough, built-to-last type of people. We are the durable beyond measure type of people. Only Brooklyn's *real* finest can embody her true hustler's spirit and pound the pavement attitude. We lived, ate, and breathed hustling.

Hustling was not just a way of life; it was a form of surviv-al. However, I look back and wonder if everyone was just too trusting, crazy, stupid, or bored to carelessly get into a van ride with strangers. Especially women! At the age of fourteen, I was all of those things. Cell phones weren't yet circulating, let alone the internet. However, I optimistically woke up every single day preparing myself for voluntary abduction.

Welcome to Brooklyn. Picturesque tree-lined streets, re-nowned for its landmarks, Brooklyn's bones are genuinely beautiful. However, whenever I reveled in her goodness, the disorder and commotion inevitably appeared without fail. If I wasn't riding my bike or admiring the landscape, I was getting thrown around in the back of a dollar van from an impromptu police chase. Good or bad, I will always love Brooklyn. While I wasn't born there, I was certainly bred there. Brooklyn doesn't just have character, it is a character. There's never a dull moment. She, Brooklyn, is a hard woman who wears leather, drinks whiskey, has instincts like a mother, uses anything as a weapon, and hangs around illegal lottery spots. But, at the same time, she is domestically inclined, knowing her way around any kitchen, loves to nurture others, and is completely family oriented. I am Brooklyn.

Growing up, there were Bloods on one block, Crips on another, and Hasidic Jews all in between. Culturally rich, Brooklyn offered authentic Chinese, Jamaican-Chinese, and even Trini-Chinese restaurants. Nostalgic West Indian scents of roti, pholourie, bake and saltfish, jerk and sorrel, waft from every block, corner, or backyard.

Even with the same cuisine on every block, I never got the sense that they were in competition. There are tons of West Indian restaurants in Flatbush. I had my favorites and wouldn't hesitate to travel to them — all the while obtaining street cred along the way. Flatbush, Crown Heights, Bed-Stuy, and Brownsville are all the places where I'd have to fight to keep the sneakers that I had on, or the coat that I was wearing. There were times when I barely missed a bullet due to my lack of discipline and the lethal rebuttals that I kept in my pocket. Though I had access to many, I didn't carry a gun, but most of my friends did. I knew that my father would put me under the jail if he ever found me carrying a piece.

Despite it all, Brooklyn was the place to be — where I loved to go to the mom and pop sneaker shops and boost Guess from Kings Plaza and the Albee Square mall. I'd also hang out on Franklin Ave., the boosting headquarters of the '90s. Plenty would stand in a clotted mass of labels, accessories, and egos just longing to get chased by the police. We had a major illegal operation going on right under the cops' and our parents' noses. There was a popular department store named Bobby's where I frequently shopped. I was obsessed with buying their West Indian novelties. Whenever I had the opportunity to treat myself, I would splurge there first. Immediately upon entering, uninterested in what's on sale, I searched for bedding and pajamas. I stood in line to purchase a granny-styled fleece robe, a two-piece flannel pajama set, and a bed in a bag – nurturing the old soul in me. Ever since I was a young girl, being comfy and having fresh linens was a thing of mine. Bobby's had great options, however, as much as I loved the content inside of Bobby's Department Store, surprisingly, I couldn't stand their customer service. If only the hot commodities weren't amongst their cold dispositions. As a young teen, regardless of how often my family or I shopped, I never felt welcomed. That's that old Brooklyn West Indian flair, a little arrogance mixed with sarcasm, while they're sucking their teeth into a smirk.

I'm Panamanian. Therefore, I'm well versed in sarcasm — like all West Indians. Bobby's Department Store and Flatbush Avenue on the weekends in the 80's were my two mandatory stops.

Saturday's consisted of many families visiting the Asian fruit and vegetable markets, Bobby's, then the Kenmore movie theater. My Saturdays, however, started at my favorite cousin Lesha's house then we moved on to the infamous Kenmore Theater. The Kenmore Theater was a death trap, yet that major circumstance never had any influence on us kids or our parents. Put it this way, hopefully, you were able to make it out with what you brought in and remain unharmed. Why I would sit in the theater some days with bullets flying over my head, a man jerking off to the left of me, and rats galore running beneath my feet? I honestly have no idea.

Seven nights per week were spent at an outdated Erasmus Hall High School, followed by courses at Kingsborough Community College. Kingsborough, stunning to say the least, was the total opposite of the dilapidated Erasmus. I really appreciated the appeal of the campus but hated the distance. Going there made me realize just how big Brooklyn was. I traveled on three buses and it took over an hour to get there – all in the same borough.

Even with Brooklyn's sprawling nature, nothing would deter me from making my rounds throughout the borough as a youngster — three buses, a train, nor a dollar van would run me away. I had stuff to do and people to see. I never stood still. I enjoyed visiting the affluent areas where the fancy homes were along an infamous bike excursion. Every year, I looked forward to the annual West Indian Day Parade. I loved weaving in and out of those streets. I would tell anyone *I'm from Brooklyn!* And, honestly, just saying that alone was verification that my knowledge of anything tough was authentic. It's a silent certification that you're street smart. Being a teenager in Brooklyn in the '80s and '90s, pre-gentrification era, meant the only things that mattered were music and having a sense of fashion. It was a gritty and dangerously exciting time.

Daddy's house was all about porridge, plantains, and prudence. Porridge, because I woke up to the smell of cinnamon and cloves every single day. I would alternate between cornmeal, bananas, and oats. Plantains would be used, specifically, as a condiment for their sweetness. Ideally, plantains are a staple that accompanies most Latin or West Indian meals. Therefore, they were always around. Since I have Cuban and Panamanian ancestry, plantains were extensive. And, well, *prudence* was a term used on my dad's side for a woman's private area, something my Jamaican-Panamanian grandmother made up. Daddy was adamant that we were not hoes. He thought, "We better have the cleanest prudence ever!" So, we made sure to do both. I always tell people that my father raised a pit bull in a skirt.

My father, Alejandro, also raised a Latina princess. He and my stepmom Melinda blasted reggae, merengue, and salsa in my ears every Saturday morning. Waking up to Carlos Santana was a pleasant disturbance, but the main incentive was to get us up and out of bed to thoroughly clean the house. And I loved my father's house. It was one of the nicer homes in the neighborhood with parquet floors, eccentric furnishings of a black leather chair and red leather couch. Dad and Melinda's home had a European flare. Though tiny, my sister and I had our own rooms. We'd get up, get dressed for the day, skip the kitchen to avoid confrontation, and then vacate the premises. We knew that cleaning and attitudes were on the horizon. So, we'd lock ourselves in our rooms for hours because the floor *was wet* or we left the house for the entire day. There was no telling when we would ever return, however, we knew we couldn't come back home with guests because the place was spotless.

Melinda was a stern St. Thomian with devout loyalty who's been in my life as long as I can remember and we've butt heads for equally the same period of time. Melinda's restraint is unmatched because she's never spanked me. I could not work my magic on her — not one bit. I was so impressed knowing how hard I prodded. She'd just pinch my ear until it hurt, if I pushed too far. We'd butt heads while I was as young as Melinda was over my sister and I fairly early. We came into her life just before becoming preteens.

In my earlier years, before moving to my father's house, my sister and I lived in the first residence that I ever called home with my mother. A Co-Op on 44 Metropolitan Oval Parkchester. It was a middle-class neighborhood in the Bronx, a sweet place to live back then and it had a real community and family feel to it. Everyone was always chipping in for something — either decorations or perpetual donations.

This was the first time I saw the Salvation Army Santa that stood in front of the theaters seeking money for charity. I always looked at him with a side-eye, wondering if his gig was legit or if he was just a straight up pedophile. All Santa's looked weird or creepy to me as a child and I didn't like interacting with grown men who weren't family members anyway. I was made aware of certain behaviors and references that men do as soon as I could comprehend it. That message was instilled early. Safety instructions for my sister and I went way further than just, "don't talk to strangers." You could say that we had profiles in our minds of what creeps looked like and how they acted. Ew! The fear of my family members was a constant reminder of some darkness which lurked about as if they knew something that we didn't. It almost felt like they didn't want to reveal too much, but just enough for us to stay alert. My dad always warned us and was blatantly vocal about the inappropriate men. As a young girl he would say, "Never sit on a man's lap!" He wouldn't give any more details, directions, or explanations. When he spoke, you understood that he was alluding to no male contact period! Sadly, those same fears of being taken advantage of by a certain man would come to fruition for me in the near future. It was something that still makes the hair stand up on my dad's back and was excruciatingly hard for all of us to work through.

The '80s in New York was bustling with abuse and corruption and, unfortunately, the exploitation of it was fairly normal to witness or experience. I was definitely a victim. However, as I got older, I grasped this prevalent problem (men's inappropriate behavior). I minimized the behavior, essentially assuming that it was what most men do. Being desensitized and mentally undeveloped, I viewed myself as less of a sufferer — basically as if I wasn't human. How horrible! Nonetheless, the kids in the '80s, were really up for grabs in those days! It was as if the whole city was living in the madhouse.

Domestic violence wasn't taken seriously yet, let alone the security of a child. Clearly, this experience sent my issues into overdrive. As a child, this victimization was my first real indication of how adults can betray me. Prior to that experience, my only hardship in life was a mild punishment, like no pistachio pudding after dinner or missing out on a Charlie Brown special. Aside from Santa, the neighborhood was a charming and cute place to live in, but it was only a short stay.

My mother moved my sister and I to Harlem; signifying the end of carefree times. Harlem of the '80s was ground zero for crack. However, like most people, my mother was oblivious to this new beast. This new demon drug, crack cocaine, roared in and annihilated like an atomic bomb. It was prevalent, as was angel dust.. It was specifically introduced to criminalize Blacks and Latinos; targeting our neighborhoods with hopes to destroy it. And, it worked. It felt as if we were living among the walking dead.

However, prior to crack-infested streets, I can clearly recall that my fondest memories with my mom were created living there — in the Bronx, just before her boyfriend moved in. Moving to Harlem was not on my priority list at all as a child. I honestly loved living in the Bronx and I loved it even more because of the movie and dinner nights that my mother, my sister, and I hosted on the living room floor. We piled up blankets, bought Arthur Treacher's, and mom would bake us a 7-Up cake. But that all fizzled when she met her boyfriend who moved into the new Harlem apartment as well. At first, I assumed the pungent stench of evil he wore was just flatulence and that he would air out in about a day or so. But one week later came the same aura, the same man, and same scent of old moldy leather, rotten meat, Cafe Bustelo, and Camel cigarettes. My mother's boyfriend was no decent man. He had heavy hands that I saw go places they never ever should have gone, and he also physically made me go places unscrupulous for a child. While his heavy hands only hit my body, his commands of me seemed to be more depraved. After he was introduced, my sister and I began spending more and more time with our dad.

You see, my dad has always enjoyed the fruits of his manual labor job at Con Edison which he worked at for years. When splurging on his girls, he was unapologetic and also enjoyed the finer things in life for himself (Barney's, BMW's, tailored clothes). He seemed healthy and strong because his diet only consisted of plantains, avocados, and beans. Therefore, as a child, I looked at him the same way I did Popeye. Having an ITAL lifestyle and being plant-based was a discipline that enamored me as a young girl. My dad symbolized a new life; a life that just seemed vivacious and happy. I was basically bursting at my Sassoon seams with anticipation of living with my dad. He has always been such a strong and powerful force. So, being around him just made us feel protected. My sister and I wanted to feel that security. Therefore, in conjunction with other circumstances, between the ages of eight and ten, my sister and I went to live with him. But, even as a child, I felt torn. I was torn between doing what was right for me versus what my heart felt. I knew that my mother was in an unhealthy situation and that she needed that same protection too.

My mother, my first designated nurturer, is more than easy on the eyes. As a child, I was entranced by her beauty and captivated by the jasmine essence that she emanated. Her look was so exotic and unique that I'd stare at her and think to myself, "she is so beautiful." Then, I realized that she's actually mine — becoming territorial, giddy, and proud inside. Her blue-tinted, almond shaped eyes complimented her lush jet black, curly hair. It perfectly framed the face of her bronze, structured cheekbones. My mother, an Afro-Cuban woman, has an ethereal beauty to her that is soft and delicate; an equivalent to her personality. That's my mom — a strikingly, attractive woman with a calm air and inviting presence.

Being aesthetically perfect, she was such a huge female figure to me as a child. Despite all that existed at the time, I was proud to have her and love her. My mother was in a good space emotionally and mentally prior to meeting Mr. Evil. I clung to the memories of that person and tried to save and protect that person from harm. Coming to terms with saying good-bye to that person and facing what was about to transpire was heartbreaking for me. It's a helpless and defeated feeling when you come to the realization, as a kid, that you can't do a damn thing to save those you love. A total custodial parental change occurred, the separation anxiety on top of the regular anxiety from missing my mother was a lot to bear.

I was happy and excited for change, yet at the same time, I was enraged by the slightest smell of stress. I wanted to be less involved in adult drama and I wanted to erase all of the things that I saw and felt prior. I wanted my mother to fight for my sister and I, to show more resistance, and to show more love — something I would obsess over growing up. Having issues with my mother also affected my female relationships as I didn't know how to maintain one. I had to learn, mostly through bad experiences, how to have healthy and compassionate relation-ships with females. Overtime I've learned how compassion, understanding and relatability are all things conducive to hav-ing healthy positive female relationships.

It was difficult without my mom around. Living with my father and stepmother, I'd misconstrue Melinda's discipline for just being mean. In some cases, I needed more compassion and kindness, but she wasn't built that way. I was a bit pushy and poked for attention a great amount. I felt like I knew what I needed and that was to receive empathy and to be heard. This would be crucial and lifesaving because negative thinking was wearing me out. It eventually provoked so much self-doubt in my headspace that there was minimal room left for logic. Festering thoughts started to harbor and that quickly turned into insecurity. This became the driving force for my behavior. If I was in a situation where I thought or felt someone was being biased towards me, I would say something so obnoxious and jaw dropping just to hurt them so they could feel my pain. The fact was that I was treating people according to my thoughts and feelings rather than through a lens of reality and the truth around me.

There was some leftover shame from the insults that I received as a kid growing up in the '80s and '90s that still resided in me. Teasing me about my skin was an easy go-to, mainly due to being so scarce in the mainstream media back then. Of course, there were dark-skinned people around however, my dark (darker than average then), at that time, was minimally exposed. Dark-skinned-anything was considered dirty, ghetto, dangerous, and frankly just unattractive. Trying to pursue any kind of friendship or social life with the *dark skin monkey* on my back was very difficult for me. Overall, my skin color dictated how I was treated.

Little old me without any recourse allowed the treatment to cripple me. It was beyond hurtful. With deep resentment, I would cry to myself at times asking God to stop it. I'd say, "Put an end to the ridicule! Just make them stop and make it go away!" I'd wake up in the morning, look in the mirror and reconfirm my struggle (you're still dark — operation love myself agenda is still in full effect). Then, I'd grab another tube of self-esteem, slather on some layers of dignity and pride, in attempts to thicken my thin skin from the verbal lashing. However, it didn't work.

My skin! It was an armor of self-hate that I couldn't break out of and it was suffocating me. I remember wanting to bleach my skin when I was younger because I was mesmerized whenever a

Porcelana skin lightening cream commercial came on. I was just in awe as a little girl and would be excited and watch the entire commercial. The ad featured a white woman with blonde hair applying lotion to her hands and face. It was nothing extremely exciting, yet I was like a deer in headlights as I watched. Who knows exactly what I was thinking! But, I was definitely under a brainwashing spell if I was in a trance every single time that commercial came on. Geez! For years, through the media, Black people have been made to believe that white skin, blonde hair, and blue eyes were the epitome of beauty. So, if that was the status quo then, I was the polar opposite. I was so young when that commercial aired, but clearly, based off my behavior, I identified with not seeing much of me on television It seemed as if I had already connected my skin with being unattractive. My skin, the first thing anyone saw was grimacing to some.

My skin, the color that determined my priority most times, was overlooked. Contrary to how I stood out, at times, I was still not seen. Go figure! I now know that I was so bitter and hateful toward myself that I attracted ignorance. Oddly, I accepted the ignorance over a soothing pep talk about my ancestors and how melanin rich I was. I neglected to entertain the creepy, but appreciated, black dolls my mother handmade or bought me. It didn't matter how much black history was in my arsenal and ingrained in me. My only concern was people not liking me. Not to mention that I'm an Afro-Latina — that was a conversation that no one was ready for. So, I just rolled with the ignorance and treated people based off of my insecurity.

My mother was very inconsistent in those days and I missed her. Gratefully, Melinda was an amazing supplement. She was a great provider, like my dad. She catered to any and every event, whether it was a family event or a social affair. She cooked dinner every single night except on Friday's (her only day off). I know, for certain, that her domestic style influenced how I am with my household: Holidays, (specifically Thanksgiving), nightly dinners, her cleaning style — all of it.

My dad was a real ITAL man who adhered to a strict Jamaican Rastafarian lifestyle, before cutting his locs after over thirty years. He spoke eloquent Spanish as if he'd just docked at the Panama Canal and always deceived people because looking at him, one would believe the only thing set to come out of his mouth was, "ye mon." Yes, Spanish oozed out of my dad's mouth, it was always quite surprising.

His locs were down to the back of his thighs, before he cut them, and he stood at 6 feet tall. So, imagine the consequences of me wanting to put any sort of chemical in my hair. I desired a perm yet wearing anything that looked remotely promiscuous (or as a hoe exposing her prudence) was completely out of the question. This was all part of the lifestyle. In turn, his lifestyle became mine.

There was absolutely no junk food in the house, only fresh foods. This was the era where UTZ snacks and Domino's (Pizza Hut was only in the white hoods) were prevalent everywhere. For us, beef and broccoli were not only underneath every kitchen table, because it was on our feet, but it was on top of every kitchen table as well. We didn't question what we were served back then, and we enjoyed the grease with glee. The motto for take-out meals in the '90s was *the greasier the better*. Therefore, my dad's expectations were almost impossible to meet. Inevitably, his rules flew out the window when I went to school, especially high school because I could leave the premises for lunch.

Seward Park High School annex kept me enrolled and in attendance for about a year and a half. The annex must be specified due to the complete contrast in size and stature from its sister school. It wasn't long before I soon realized that I was in East Side High from the movie, *Lean on Me*. The only differences were that Joe Clark wasn't my principal and my school wasn't in New Jersey. The conflicts and the fighting were a part of our curriculum. I think the students actually began to schedule fights at some point, with openings as early as 7:30 AM, from the train station.

I'd often scrutinize the classroom walls. I knew for a fact that there must've been asbestos that they weren't telling us about. I'd squint with confusion, tapping my fingers while watching, waiting, and counting the paint chips as they fell from the ceiling. saying, "I've been in project buildings that had better paint jobs than this — like come on!" I firmly believe that teaching or even working at Seward Park was an easy paycheck for most - the faculty clearly didn't handle their responsibilities. My sister cut school and took a test next to me in science class. Engaging as if we were friends, we went to lunch and she came back to class with me. Nobody stopped her or even asked any questions. Anybody could walk in and do whatever they wanted. First week in, I knew I needed to have my dawgs in Brooklyn on standby at all times, you know, in case I needed them. Having my cousins or my homegirls there to assist me in keeping my reputation intact was big business. I had zero losses.

However, there were too many gangs in Seward Park. These particular groups of people would hold each other down. In other words, they secured and monopolized certain areas, establishing invisible boundaries that others respected. The annex was heavily segregated by ethnicity. The inevitably existing black and white biases were something that I was familiar with, but I was not acquainted with the others. My school was located in the LES (Lower East Side). Naturally, we had Latino cliques. However, it was the Asian cliques that impressed me. The Asians moved in large groups and looked serious while doing so. Ironically, there weren't any rivalries amongst anyone, but it was quite clear whose territory we were in. Asian territory! I left Seward High in the middle of my sophomore year and went to obtain a GED. I couldn't take it anymore. With the environment unattended, unsupervised, and unsanitary, I was destined for failure. My mother, the philosophical doc, basically lived in Teachers College at Columbia University, where she studied. And so, that is where I went to study for a month to prepare. I took my GED at sixteen and aced it on my first try. I felt so established after that. I was elated from what I had accomplished all on my own, it felt great. However, as soon as I left school, I had to return once again. I was only allowed to take my GED contingent upon going straight to college. So, I enrolled in Kingsborough Community College, hoping to prioritize my future.

Though the Flatbush streets would ultimately keep me hostage. They called my name and brought me back like a boomerang. An experience similar to that of my first romance.

Growing up, I never understood what love really was. I'm not talking about love at its surface, I'm talking about the depth of love. I always knew I was cared for. But as for love, the definition and the act, it was never proclaimed as an action. I never perceived it as something that someone did or something that happened. I perceived it as something that someone said. Even though it was said often, I was never given a fundamental explanation of what it actually was. Yes, my parents always said that they loved me, but I received that as something they had to say. I thought that it was just a routine—something that parents should tell their children. It wasn't until I became rebellious and

when I put them in uncomfortable predicaments which caused them to force discipline on me, that I began to see their version of what love was. Most times, it was pleasant and at other times, it wasn't. Either way, my genuine idea of what love was, at that time, consisted of words that you wrote on a card for the people who you cared for.

CHAPTER 3

An Illegible Start to Love

I met Mike when I was fourteen years old. He spotted me on the streets of Brooklyn, eyed and complimented my Columbia jacket, then walked me home. I thought it was the sweetest thing. He was seventeen and came from a large Guyanese family from Brooklyn too. We were young, dumb and crazy in lust. With Mike, I fell into my first real relationship that went on to last for four years. There were many hot and heavy times as we deeply immersed ourselves into this thing called romance. We were inseparable. So much so, that I found myself homeless. My father, the patriarch, was not ready to see his youngest girl so twirled into a young man. I was willing to get into all sorts of trouble for him and so I did, but Alejandro was not having it. Not only did he put me out, but he contacted all my potential housing options and told them not to take me in. I'd become a handful, but I was just enough for Mike and his family.

Mike's mother opened her door for me to stay with them for a period of time. Her liberal lifestyle helped further our young agenda. Just shy of nineteen years old, I became pregnant.

Tai, my little Panamanian, Cuban, and Guyanese blessing from God, was born on Día de Los Reyes, in 1995. Three Kings

Day, an annual international celebration on January 6th, which celebrates the occurrence of the Magi giving gifts honoring the Divinity of baby Jesus. This is when my journey into motherhood began.

I moved back with my Panamanian warrior father, Alejandro, and Melinda, in the Flatbush section of Brooklyn. My older sister, who had given birth at eighteen, was also living there with her baby.

Toward the end of my pregnancy, I went back to live with my mom in the Van Cortlandt section of the Bronx. My father would say he wasn't dealing *wit him daughta*. I can still hear his rough voice. This hard-working Con Edison engineer with A1 credit wasn't about to have his two daughters ruin his legacy. He just about had it with the both of us at that point. Though I wasn't too sure why because he had his first child in Panama when he was sixteen — some nerve. My father didn't have the ideal relationship with his parents growing up. So, in a strange way, I understood him. His upbringing created cracks in his infrastructure due to a rough childhood and he was afraid of his children having the same experiences as him.

In all sincerity, my sister and I were late with baby fever compared to all our friends. Our thought process at the time was to find a good-looking mate (especially from the corner bodega, cause they have the best picks), have a baby, dress it up in expensive shoplifted clothing, and play house while living at home with no one working. That was a recipe for disaster. And, that was my cocktail.

In Van Cortlandt, my mother had a one-bedroom apartment located upstairs in a private house. She was very supportive, at this time, and excited to prepare for her second grandchild. I was touched because it was more effort from her part than I had seen in a while. This attentiveness wasn't the kind that I was used to. She bought a red crib, other new baby items, and even chose to sleep in the living room as she changed her bedroom into a nursery.

It was during a severe snowstorm when Tai would begin her entrance into the world. The conditions were horrible, and I was so nervous to go out and drive. My mother began to count the minutes between each contraction before we began the two-hour drive from the Bronx to Brooklyn. Although the pain was excruciating, I managed well and within an hour after arriving at the hospital, I gave birth. I can only compare the feeling of birthing a child to something like running a yearlong marathon. I was completely winded, dizzy, and my legs felt like noodles. It was overexertion to the fullest. Thankfully, I didn't have a long labor and all of my parts were still intact, which was such a relief! I hadn't processed what holding this little human had meant just yet. I hadn't grasped the significance of what my child represented to me and for me. It was just an experience that adults had — something I did and had to now monitor.

I was clearly disconnected from motherhood and my life overall. Nonetheless, Tai was born at Methodist Hospital, which was on the other side of town. Located in Park Slope, it's still considered one of the most affluent neighborhoods in Brooklyn.

Rooming at my mother's apartment began to wear thin. She was used to living alone, so it definitely became *Three's a Crowd*. I was so focused on perfecting my image as a new mother, that I had totally neglected to address the traumatic boats that were docked in my head. All the thoughts regarding my mother from childhood were still there, waiting for me to address them, but I didn't at the time. I had qualms that I wanted to discuss with my mother as there were some things that I needed clarity on. However, time just wouldn't agree to permit such discussions. My personal agreement (a mental and emotional pact I had created to honor myself by any means necessary), was for her to spend bonding time with my daughter in lieu of the time I missed growing up. I knew that a conversation, an apology or an understanding, regarding the past had to occur, but I wasn't sure when.

After three months of living with my mom, I optimistically returned to Brooklyn. I had to get back to my home, which was also my dad's place. After all, this was where my things were, and where my life was. Tai and I went back to Flatbush to embark on a weird and uncomfortable journey of motherhood. I really had no clue what to do and followed the actions of my friends, along with whatever maternal instinct I had. Mike's family was also around but that only lasted for so long. Mike and I were in lust, but we were not in love and the relationship wasn't right for me. My stomach wouldn't settle, let alone my brain. I was always anxious and wanted us to work out. But the reality was that we were not on the same wavelength as I worked two jobs and Mike often stayed on the streets. And thus, the relationship ended allowing me to explore my freedom once again.

CHAPTER 4

Stumbling Upon Forever

At nineteen, I may have been a young mother, but I was also still a teen looking for a life that came with fun, love and adventure. I'd find it with my home girl Inga, better known as Foxy Brown, who was a great play aunt to Tai. Inga would take me along with her to Daddy's House, Puff's recording studio for sessions. At that age, it seemed like hip hop lived and breathed among us. Busta Rhymes lived right around the corner and on any given day Special Ed could be found hanging out at my friend Amina's house. We'd all find ourselves at the Galaxy Diner on Pennsylvania Avenue. It was the place to be — to hang out, chill after the club or just to see your crew. At the time, we were all young and still discovering ourselves.

Now that Mike and I were ending, I pursued a romantic relationship with David Styles Aka Styles P, Holiday, Holiday Styles, SP, SP the ghost, Ghost and G-Host. I heard him on a few mixtapes that had me nodding my head saying, "I want him!" There was an immediate connection for me through his music. He referenced too many things that were relevant to me.

It was as if he had hidden cryptic messages just for me to decode. I was so intrigued by his music and depth that I had to meet him.

I initially met Styles at Daddy's House. I was in a session down the hall with Foxy as she recorded tracks for her debut, *Ill Nana*. She and I had been running around thick as thieves. Styles and I ran into each other in the studio and from the moment he complimented my neon nail polish, we had a connection. This was the beginning of my jet setting days and when we had downtime, Inga loved spending time with Tai. She absolutely adored my daughter as if she were her own. Inga had some of the same features that Tai had — high cheekbones, slanted eyes, and long wavy hair. So, she took an affinity to Tai immediately. Since she lived in runway clothes and had everything at her fingertips; buying Tai her first fur was a no brainer for her. In fact, she insisted. This was something that I refused to do. I think Tai was almost two at the time. But as Inga and I drifted apart over the years, Styles became a bigger fixture in my life.

Tai and I moved to Harlem as Styles became my leading man. He told me that my father shouldn't be the provider for my child and I. Styles exuded independence and he wanted the same for me. He once told me, "You need to be more independent, period!" It was strong and sexy talk. As a Pisces woman, it was also what I liked about him. It was also a real trek for Styles to come from Westchester to Brooklyn.

He traveled all that way to visit, just to end up sitting on the front steps because there were no adults at home. Some days I'd sit on the steps with Amina, whom I considered my big sister, smoking Capri cigarettes as I anxiously waited for Styles to join me.. He joined in the conversation, but not the smoking because he detested stogie smoke and still does. His emotions were a mixture of happy and annoyed at the same time. Sitting on the stoop looking idiotic together in the cold, he turned to me and said, "I can't continue to do this. I'm grown."

I could understand where he was coming from and applied his advice immediately! Though I had a child and was over nineteen, my parents' rules applied when you lived in their household. Therefore, I had to respect my dad and Melinda's agenda. I already had a child and I didn't want to rock the boat anymore. Plus, I had already experienced a small dose of what being homeless was like. Styles, on the other hand, had been on his own since he was 16. He was helping to support his brother and sister alongside his mom Daphne.

Styles came into my life and introduced me to stability, responsibility, and a great work ethic. And I introduced him to a world outside of himself. Being Cuban, I took Styles to a Cuban-Chinese restaurant and he often responded, "What is this you are bringing me to?" It was a real culture shock. I'd also take him to museums and introduce him to things he'd never experienced before. Styles and I would also sit on the phone for seven to eight hours, especially when he was on tour. We would call each other before Soul Train came on at 11am and laughed so hard at the dancers coming down the line. We wouldn't hang up until mid-morning the following day. We were friends for eight months before any physical romance and I fell hard.

Living with Tai at my dad's house just made me push harder to move out because of all the stipulations and lack of liberty. My father had the nerve to tell me that I couldn't sleep out, even though I was a grown woman with a child. My sister had already left, so that was my incentive to leave as well. However, living with and being raised by my dad was one of the best experiences of my life. I attained a solid foundation from my dad and Melinda. I respect, admire, and love that man to the moon and back. I respect, admire, and commend Melinda for accepting someone else's children and not giving up through trying times. For my dad, it takes courage and a lot of love for a man to raise two girls. As for my mother, she picked up where she left off with her granddaughter, she made a conscious effort to bond.

Growing up too fast was seemingly always on my agenda. Perhaps it's that darn old soul in me. So, I continued to challenge myself and moved out of my father's home. Following in my sister's footsteps, I went to the same place that she moved to. I knew that I had to leave. Styles was definitely an incentive to get me moving and shaking. I was excited to start our journey together. The thought of moving was so overwhelming and gave me anxiety knowing that daddy was no longer in the next room. Nonetheless, I had absorbed so much growing up in Brooklyn, in conjunction with numerous branches that I've spawned from the steady trunk of my dad. Brooklyn was the survival of the fittest. And, I survived.

CHAPTER 5

Lady in Bloom

Free at last! Free at last! Thank God Almighty!

At the age of twenty-one, being in Harlem in the late '90s on the brink of the millennium was so liberating for me as a new adult. My sentiments regarding Harlem's appeal obviously changed since I was a child. With gentrification in its embryo faze it was a new Harlem World. It was an abrupt move from home, and it provided the jolt I needed; paving the road for my independence. Ironically, the feelings of emancipation were constantly being chased by bewilderment. My mind would go, "You're in way over your head! You jumped all the way out of the window with this one. Okay, so you know that you're not even close to being financially stable right?" It always led me to ultimately say, "I can't believe I'm leaving Brooklyn." However, after my sister and I were robbed for the 100th time, this time at gunpoint with my niece in the stroller, I knew that a change of location would definitely be good.

I was free from the constraints of a parent, yet I was so confused and scared of this new feeling of freedom, also known as adulthood. From my vantage point, my developmental process was in an erratic, foggy, and overall difficult stage. It was difficult for me to see a clear purpose and path to navigate. Ultimately, this pattern led me toward decisions that weren't so smart.

Tai had begun daycare in Harlem near the Polo grounds. This is where I really noticed my dynamic daughter was going to be a bit of a challenge for me, just like I was for my parents. I had a lot of impromptu learning to adjust to along with having to understand that children are individuals. Not all children are the same in terms of their learning styles and behavior. This was something extremely hard for me to understand at first. It meant that I had to delve into areas of psychology that I'd had no prior knowledge. At twenty-one, I didn't have a blueprint because there simply isn't one! What's good for some may not be best for all kids. This was something that I had to learn through research. I later grasped from the school's occupational therapist that Tai learned and retained better in a smaller setting. The therapist advised that I manipulate her class schedule one year so that I could get her in smaller groupings. So, I did just that. Thankfully, I saw dramatic results. Nonetheless, Tai displayed such a determination for what she wanted earlier on. She was basically showing me that I had my own damn self on my hands and thus I could accurately panic for the future. I knew exactly what I was working with, a miniature me.

My move to Harlem wasn't alone. I moved with my girlfriend Danielle, aka Miss Bowlegs, along with her son Dimitri. Dannie was the perfect roommate because she came from a very respectful and responsible household in Brooklyn, like mine. She lived on Carroll Street in Crown Heights along with her family. Now, we had moved to 140th between 7th and 8th together. We settled into a cozy two bedroom walk up on the 4th floor. We both roomed with our kids and, conveniently, they played together. We cooked, cleaned, and smoked a lot of weed. I began smoking weed at the age of seventeen recreationally with friends and it became a great way to escape for a moment. It was our real *wow, we are grown* moment and we took full advantage of it. Growth was slower back then. Dannie and I did the best that we could with the knowledge we had. It was truly survival! Our kids were in daycare, so we weren't that negligent. As highly medicated as we were, we ate until we were sick of ourselves and kneeled over from having the munchies. It was hilarious because one of us would cook a whole spread Thanksgiving style. The other one would salivate from anticipation; waiting for the finished product — a totally unnecessary adolescent routine. We were hungry for sure, but not hungry enough to feed five firefighters. Fat cow is the nickname we liked to call each other. I'd ask, "Feeling like a fat cow?" Depending on the answer, we'd stop or continue eating. We were definitely low lives, behind closed doors, at that time. We were only twenty-one and twenty-three years old and it was our first taste of freedom. It could have been way worse.

Our parents were convinced that we were living a *Sex and The City* lifestyle as professionals working a 9-5, but it was quite the opposite. We were straight up hustlers! But Dannie and I were raised to have discipline. Therefore, we were very conservative with our drama and we were on the very lower end of the totem pole of hustling. We had to be disciplined to a degree — our parents were strict and neither one of us wanted to answer to them. Nonetheless, Dannie and I always kept legitimate odd jobs. However, we didn't work too often. She went the legal route, whereas mine was riskier, yet s legit. My paycheck, however, was rendered under the table.

One of my odd jobs, at that time, was at an art gallery in Brooklyn. Though, I stopped working there just as soon as I started because I wasn't making much money, I did love the freedom that it gave me and how much it kept me occupied while Tai was in school. I managed the gallery in a beautiful brownstone in Crown Heights. I have always been a creator, a painter, a sculptor, and artist since youth and accepting that job required minimal thought. However, I was bored. I was a receptionist, consultant, and assistant. I was unenthusiastic even with having all of those titles. Plus, I was a young mother. The only fitting position left for me in the world would have been professional hustling. I quit and became a full-time parent with a little bit of hustling on the side. I was hanging with the wrong people. It wasn't the baby boomers era then. It was the identity theft era. The birth of the credit card crazies. The impact that it had on the streets was so powerful. It had become so popular that one would have thought it was a legitimate career and so I dabbled. God said to me, "So you want to meddle with your freedom? And, you're willing to travel to do it? Okay." He took me on an unexpected trip to an island. Rikers Island. This was not part of the plan at all. It was a huge hiccup and a huge disruption in my flow of life — all from being in the wrong place at the wrong time.

There weren't any better or worse parts about the experience. The whole thing stunk — literally. The abominable stink from the tombs (central booking) and Rikers were so thick that I felt as though it stained my clothes and skin. It felt like I'd walked straight into a Petri dish. The walls, bars, and floors are lacquered with whatever death smells like — metal, urine, and that angel dust again. It was dark and lifeless despite all the bodies that are housed there. Hence, the word *tomb*, that holds the deceased, makes me wonder where the actual name of the jail originated. The smell and overall experience were enough to keep me from even dreaming about being in jail ever again. Styles was on tour and I didn't want to be scolded by my sister. So, I called my dad to bail me out. It was embarrassing to say the least. Luckily, I had enough money saved for him to use and didn't need a loan. That would not have been good for me because I would have owed more than money — I would have owed my life. Rikers was a one and done experience! I was only in jail and hustling part-time because I felt financially insecure. I'd found out that Styles and I were pregnant. I wanted to cover all bases. I had another kid on the way and, to be honest, I wasn't sure if the relationship or the money would be stable. So, I did what I knew. I hustled. The extra gig was for paying bills, not flossing.

Consistent money was still a bit of a challenge. Mike was vaguely in the picture. He'd appear from time to time. And, if he wasn't, his sister was. When my shared lease with Dannie expired, I moved back to the Bronx. Harlem was such a short stay. The memories that remain include becoming pregnant with my son, eating Copeland or M&G's every single day, and smoking copious amounts of weed.

Styles, my daughter, and my pregnant self were all moving again. This time we were moving as a family. A main incentive for the move was simply Styles' growing popularity. His rap group, The LOX, was everywhere and they were gaining huge success. As a result, living on 140th street was not the best option.

We moved to Riverdale, New York into the cutest two-bedroom, stabilized, walk-up apartment. It was right across from Van Cortlandt Park which was perfect for my children. Tai had her own room. It was quite big, and it overlooked the park. This was the time that she created her own uniforms at home. She religiously wore a denim dress with a yellow and red floral swimsuit underneath. She'd come home, pull the clothes out of her trunk, immediately strip and put that 'fit on. Too funny and too cute! She was a busy little lady. Someone was always picking her up for something, whether it was a baby shower or a birthday. She was certainly busier than her parents. Tai was booked on the weekends. My friend Tiffany, another person who was privileged to be in Tai's life, was basically her captor. Tai was a human doll to her. She had parties lined up for the whole year just so she could take Tai, show her off and prance around with her. And Tai loved it. Tiffany had her own name for Tai. It was so bizarre, but she did! Tai had several nicknames: Tai Tai, My Tai, and Tai Tai Strawberry. But Tiffany called her Taiisha. and I actually agreed to that for decades. If Tai wasn't with her, then she was with my sister, mother, or Mike too.

Though we'd moved to the Bronx, we were still traveling back to Harlem for daycare twice a day so that I could maintain some sort of stability with her schooling and because my niece attended the same school too. Tai and her cousin were like sisters from birth. I wanted to keep it that way by always encouraging and supporting their bond. If my kids received thirty Christmas gifts each, Asia was afforded the same luxury.

I had gotten somewhat adjusted to this new rental, then Noah was born. Noah Thamsanqua Styles, brother to Tai, was born on May 26, 1998 — my little Noah aka Noodles or Little Avocado (as my mom calls him). He was so special when he was born, for the mere fact that boys were scarce in our family. Spoiling him was immediate and encouraged. Tai, however, wasn't enthused. The two eventually became so vital to each other over time. They were inseparable. They were the most important people in each other's lives. Tai, from the beginning, was extremely overprotective of her brother. You know the expression *Only I can make my brother cry, not you.* That was Tai! Noah stayed in awe of his big sister. She could do no wrong. He was behind Tai like a shadow; adjusting to each other was an easier transition for the kids than it was mine, as a parent. That sh*t was hard. Both Tai and the baby wanting all of my attention plus having insecurities with my then boyfriend had me feeling overwhelmed. I miserably existed then, hanging on by a thread. I wanted out of my reality some days because the responsibilities often seemed too much.

In search of some solid ground after Noah was born, I went to culinary school. It was a way for me to delve back into my creativity through food. Tai was three going on four and Noah was anywhere between six to eight months old. I attended a one-year program at The New York Restaurant School. I felt like I finally had control of my life and its path. I could attain something that no one could take away from me, education and knowledge. However, I had quit six months in. I just couldn't swing it all. Styles was a new rapper who still had some misogynistic tendencies left. He was still young-minded and very unbalanced as well. Infidelity escapades in conjunction with him continuously on the road touring eventually took a toll and I just couldn't swing it all. Though both of our parents were around and very supportive, I still couldn't push through. The academic work was so intimidating and gave me so much anxiety that I eventually gave up. I figured that I would just be cooking in school. What does math and science have to do with cooking anyway? The work probably wasn't very difficult, but overthinking can make anything impossible. In addition, I wasn't emotionally prepared to handle the workload, a toddler, an infant, and run a household. It was one of the hardest decisions for me to make; sacrificing a professional career over my family.

An overwhelming repetitiveness of parenting, fulfilling wifey duties and not living for myself had stress oozing out of me and I was over it. I wanted out of my reality. Yes, I could run away, but where was I going? Sometimes I'd think to myself I should call someone but my pride always overrode having any conversation. I constantly felt as though my stress was heightened by the slightest peak of sensibility. I eagerly took a bottle of Advil to the face in hopes to fatally succeed in getting out of here — or so I had thought! God had other plans for me. Oddly, after the regurgitating had subsided, I eventually calmed down. I could hear angels speak to me. Their intervention, along with an ache in my throat, would help me realize not to sweat the small stuff. Instead, it taught me to breathe and to think of my kids. I thought, what would happen to them? What would they think of me? The monumental feelings of anxiety and anger along with all of the voices preaching negatively like Crazy Eddie in my head were totally diminished. I am not saying that those feelings didn't exist. I'm just saying that I understood whatever I was going through wasn't that serious. Foolishly and uncomfortably sitting on the floor while cuddling the toilet, I was then able to harness my emotions. With the bitter taste of Advil residue and shame in mouth, I actually got clarity and saw some light. Drowsy, sweaty, and fatigued because throwing up non-stop is like a serious cardio workout, I took a nap; vowing to never share this experience. I remember trying to doze off in a lethargic tranquil state admittedly telling myself not to act stupid just for attention. I have never been able to make the right decisions while being under an angry state of mind. I'm too impulsive; something I'm working on. Either way, nothing should ever be that serious for me to attempt to take a life, especially my own. I realized that it is more of a looming anger issue that needed handling, rather than me actually not wanting to exist.

～

It seemed as though trying to run before learning how to walk was the method that Styles and I used in life. The preliminary stages of business and parenting were taxing times. There was a lot of trial and error. We saw the finish line and we knew our potential, but we didn't have the right tools to execute it yet. There was no fundamental understanding or references when it came to managing our finances. We had no clear answer on how to raise kids either. We definitely attended a trial and error for dummies class for a few years. There is no manual for life.

There was Disturbia in Suburbia aka the Styles family. With Styles growing his profile as a rapper, we went from Bad Boy money to Ruff Ryder money. It was coming in left and right. Styles and I dived right into real estate by purchasing our first home. We bought a townhouse in White Plains and I felt so grown at such a young age. Expensive trips anywhere became our new lifestyle. We went to the United Arab Emirates. We went to Ireland, Croatia, and even Norway. We began purchasing a new car each quarter — surround sound and everything! The hottest designers and jewelers were adorning us. For a moment, it seemed as though all our troubles had disappeared. Life was great, yet somehow, through all of this, we forgot we had children to take care of and we needed to save for rainy days. We realized we needed a better overall plan for the future. Yes, we had life insurance, bank accounts and college funds. However, we were still spending erroneously — a real detriment!

Neither one of us were raised with the kind of money that we had coming in. Money management was one of the many courses that we were thrusted into learning. And boy oh boy did we learn! Having money doesn't mean that one knows how to adequately spend it. Maybe one knows how to spend it, but we didn't know how to prioritize it. The first property we purchased in White Plains was a three bedroom, three bathroom townhome. I was twenty-three and he was twenty-five — very, very young. The kids had a great set up. There was custom furniture, bedrooms with intricate hand-painted borders that were all painted by me; with all the trimmings. There were big picturesque windows with animated stickers that I applied and changed weekly. There were parties that were planned months ahead with details too infinite to imagine — like the cake that I baked to match the interactive Spider-Man I hired, which was climbing and flying throughout my home. I made a model cake after him, consisting of a spider that scaled a building and then flew to the streetlight. I was always knee deep in it. There were never dry, dull moments with my kids. If I wasn't being entertained or exasperated from their cackling personalities, then most likely, they were entertaining themselves. My kids had access to game devices prior to them being released. Noah and Tai had a plethora of entertaining options. You name it, they had it. Therefore, they were always occupied.

Noah was still at home while Tai was enrolled in public school. She enjoyed school when she was actually participating and learning, but if her mind wasn't being stimulated, then Tai felt bored. If Tai could have it her way, her school day would only consist of art, science, and gym class. If a subject wasn't of much interest to her then you could forget about any interaction from her. She didn't have attention deficit disorder because I had her tested. She was just that headstrong. She'd rather have a conversation with an adult than one of her peers. It was more entertaining and interesting for Tai. I honestly was the same as her growing up. So, that willfulness attitude was no stranger to me. Just like Tai, I was extremely intelligent and very determined. Tai, as diligent as she was, immediately took a liking to all things artsy. That was when I realized she had the same disease that I had. Blankaphobia. This was the fear of leaving anything untampered — blank. Decorating things was our signature way to personalize anything. I get excited after purchasing anything bare because, until then and in my mind, it's still not really mine. The love of all arts was another trait we shared. It didn't matter if it was performing in a play, a band, or an art project, she was all in, which meant that the whole family was in.

Whether enthused or not, if Tai needed a partner to practice with and you were around, you were automatically a willing participant to her. One could be there for hours because Tai would definitely maximize her time with you. As a family, our household was saturated with music. As a result, we were always competing for ear space, especially on the weekends. Billie Joe Armstrong and Green Day were my extended family for about five years. Every family member of ours was well-versed in their backstory, families, and album sales. Tai was obsessed with a wide range of artists. Therefore, if you were in close proximity of her those days not only were you a forced participant, but you'd be forced to enjoy all of her music as well.

Nirvana, Red Hot Chili Peppers, and Sex Pistols were in constant rotation, while simultaneously playing Yelawolf, Jill Scott, and Badu. Ironically, I had a real knack for alternative bands when I was her age as well. I listened to the same genres.

Since finances were increasing and stable, I felt mature and like I was on the real road to adulthood. It actually provoked an urge in me to domesticate. I decided to become a housewife of Westchester and Styles and I got engaged. I'd kept the topic of marriage up for as long as I could remember, and he knew that it was what our future held. And so, once Styles was financially free, we bought a ring. While most things seemed to be going well, trying to maintain a household, with a fiancé and two small kids was extremely difficult. I had absolutely no clue or idea about what was needed or what it took to be a great mother — keep in mind that I was a tomboy growing up. So, having a son was quite easy. There really wasn't much to do. Boys don't require much of anything. I just smiled and loved Noah to death and whatever else I thought he needed, or I had doubts about, I could just ask his dad to assist me.

With Tai, however, when it came to dealing with emotions of any kind, it was extremely challenging. I hadn't really bonded with many women. So, I was dumbstruck in this department. In addition, I still lacked some femininity to a degree. I didn't necessarily have the harmonious relationship with my mother or sister. All of us were still running from our reflections at that time — ignorant to the effects from it. I was a real fish out of the water. And, that's a horrible element for a Pisces to be in.

Trying to gauge Tai's emotions amidst an issue and make sense of them was cryptic for me—especially without being able to communicate with Mike or any of his family. It was like the twilight zone. The only member accessible was Tai's aunt (Mike's sister). Her presence was still vaguely around. Mike and his mom were involved with Tai during her younger years, however, once he and I could no longer communicate, it seemed as if no one else would either. All I had access to was her aunt, though she had three of her own kids and could not replace the absence of her brother in Tai's life, especially when Tai knew that he existed and knew that he now had other children. Nonetheless, the inconsistency was consistent. Therefore, I took whatever supplement I could get. Tai would hang out with her aunt from time to time and she seemed to really enjoy it.

I was still growing too, still figuring myself out. I was exploring and researching my own family. Hence, I was in a place of connecting as many dots as possible. I was completely detached from Mike's side, no longer aware of any genetics, history or family trauma that may have existed.

I had nothing to gauge on how to successfully build a family or home. Some words of advice: if you plan on having children, please, do yourself a favor and observe your partner's family. Make a list of the pros and cons. Get as much family history as possible. This is crucial. What good is it for the child if the parents aren't communicating but you, the mother, aren't aware that there are conditions in the family? You need to be aware of conditions, such as mental illness, high blood pressure, and even diabetes. You have nothing to go on. And, that's what I had. Surely, I knew Mike's family on the surface, but I could not call them up with my concerns and have a full-blown conversation or dig deep into their history. I had to work with the knowledge that I already had and the patterns that I already saw. There was no judgement because we all have our issues within our own families. Mike and his biological father, from my knowledge and vantage point, had zero relationship.

I could see that Tai had difficulty in a school setting early on. She'd rather be in nature, creating a painting, than to be around any immature person her age. Whatever issues she had, I struggled with learning how to handle maturely. Unfortunately, everything was a nuisance for me. I'm sure that she picked that up. For example, her first encounter with porn on the internet. It was two girls and one cup to be exact. I had no clue what it was. Being the non-discriminatory, all inclusive prankster that Tai was, she couldn't keep such an atrocity to herself, so she showed her brother as well. I watched it and then lost it. I didn't realize the curiosity — it was all normal and that I could have been composed and discussed it. I guess I had a faint fear, somewhere deep in my subconscious, of her becoming a porn-star and that outweighed any real logic. I was always in a hurry those days, overthinking to a quick resolve, which ten times out of ten always exasperated the situation.

Tai was also still in the preliminary stages of accepting her little brother and Styles. Tai never called Styles, daddy, until about six or seven years old. She just wouldn't. There was no pressure to as well, though I had formally introduced the option to her. I even nonchalantly threw the word daddy around, hoping that she'd follow suit like her brother. However, being coerced is something that Tai detested.

My guess was that she was exercising her rights after realizing she didn't have to, which was actually adorable and interesting to witness. It was interesting because Tai was innocent yet coherent anytime the opportunity to say daddy arose. It was as if every time she said David, instead of daddy, I heard, "I have an iron will." She was steadfast and consistent regarding it—which was a real confirmation and pure example of her determination Little Miss Tai settled into calling him by his first name—David. It was the same way for me, realizing that I didn't have to call Melinda, mommy at that age.

One day, Tai called Styles daddy. Styles and I just looked at each other with a blank stare but said nothing. Trying not to lock eyes for too long, we quickly and casually resumed what we were doing. I'm sure that Tai knew she had gotten our attention, but either way, we didn't want to make a huge deal about it. It is similar to when a child falls down. In the moment that a parent focuses on the booboo, it becomes more dramatic and present. We didn't want to make daddy, *too present*, so that she might consider changing her mind.

Tai is truly something else. She is some kind of wonderful! Her graceful, physical presence touched everyone she met, until you got on her bad side — a bad side that was easily penetrable. Tai and I were so alike, just like myself, she would come across as fuming with anger, but she would turn around and offer to cook a meal for you. When she was upset, she still wouldn't want anyone to starve — no matter how angry she was. At that point, everyone would be smiling again. She really couldn't stay mad for long, which probably explains why she had a lot of fans. They probably knew how to extract her golden smile too. Fans is what she called them, but in an endearing way. She was adored.

Her teachers wanted to take her home as their own child — either that or kick her out of the class for utilizing her sassy pie hole. It was either or — no gray areas with Tai. She was assertive, she knew what she wanted and wasn't afraid to get it. Like myself, Tai the artist. Charcoal, pottery, or makeup, you can take your pick. She could do it all. She created masterpieces from an early age. I still have her sketches/portraits, ceramics of elephants and mugs; not to mention her baby teeth and first haircut. I collected them all.

Tai displayed her feelings habitually and openly. It was easy for her to get hurt. A sleeve would be safer. However, she wore her heart like a down puffer coat — it protruded and was intrusive sometimes because it was bold, smothering, and it inspired thought. Tai was particular with her attention. Meaning the attention, she gave was tailored to everyone's needs. Tai's heart and her feelings basically led the way. She always went that extra mile — doing and saying that extra thing to express how much she cared about someone. She literally aimed to please. That's great, but not so great, when pleasing others becomes detrimental to oneself. For my daughter, it unfortunately led to depression from the unfulfilled expectations of others. But even the bumps in the road didn't stop Tai from building relationships with teachers, her peers, and anyone else who she felt like she had a connection with—which was great because that dynamic was quite different when she was younger.

As she grew in size and beauty, she also grew in popularity. Tai had an assortment of friends — everywhere. Oddly enough, her friends and associates were always older than her. It was weird at first, but then I just got used to it. I definitely wasn't in any position to judge the age of Tai's company, especially if the relationships were platonic because when I was twelve, I dated a twenty-two-year-old. Therefore, I was definitely mindfully aware — however, I wasn't too judgmental. On top of that, I was fearful of history repeating itself. So, I was totally okay with a two to three-year age gap. Plus, the relationships were positive. Tai's friends truly cared for her. I had to embrace them.

In retrospect, my children's idiosyncrasies and erratic cur-veballs became a distraction from what I was really enduring. I guess I enjoyed the diversion as a deflection. It prevented me from seeing the real focus at that time, which I believe was to just simply slow down. All mothers, especially young atten-tive ones, can attest to running around like chickens with their heads cut off most days — we are always running from pillar to post. We are always doing the most and accommodating ev-eryone. We always remember ourselves last. We forget that we are the spine of the family and of the house. Without us there is neither. *That was me.* My daily agenda read, "be of service mind, body, and soul to everyone else but yourself." The free-dom I was so eager to receive once leaving my father's home seemed to be suffocating me as I made my own. It was time I learned how to breathe for *myself* as well as my family.

CHAPTER 6

Standing through the Trials

Usually, my children would be the ones who woke me up. However, on this day, I was woken up by the continuous sound of my fiancé's vibrating beeper. It was an inquisitive alert, at best, due to the redundancy and the time of the pagers. My first thought was, *I'm the only one who has the authority and audacity to insist on communication around here.* It was a red flag. I'm a light sleeper so I hear everything. It is a gift and a curse. But, surprisingly, he didn't hear a thing, which was bizarre for how vigorous the vibrations were. I delicately slid over to the edge of the bed and peeled the duvet back, grabbing the beeper off the nightstand. I did a fast, but light-footed, tiptoe scurry into the bathroom. I moved like air because I had to avoid the possible noise that the cracks in the foundation could make — all the while peeking over my shoulder. The thoughts in my head said, *I am not the one.* At first glance, I knew the contact was a female. Men don't have the time or the energy to page someone numerous times back to back. I've learned only a woman does that!

I still couldn't confirm anything just yet. I jotted the number down for future reference which was in three minutes. I crept out of the bathroom like a ninja and placed the beeper back on the nightstand. Then, I headed downstairs to begin my investigation. Hot and furious, all still prematurely, I went to the kitchen, blocked my number and I called. A female answered, and I immediately hung up. Confirmed! My fiancé's cheating behavior was now established. I instinctively knew, by her sexy tone and how she overzealously answered on the first ring. She was hoping her knight was on the other end.

With no questions and no sensibility in sight, I charged back upstairs. I leapt onto the bed, where he was still in a sweet sound slumber, nestled like a baby in our Ralph Lauren damask-print sheets and whaled my fists on his head and back. Startled, he woke up and we tussled until I grew tired and fell on the floor. We weren't coherent nor could we communicate. Feeling defeated, agitated, and extremely angry, I bolted down the stairs to the kitchen, grabbed a knife and went into the powder room. Sobbing, I locked the door, and I stabbed myself in the stomach. I wasn't able to calculate how wide or how deep I went. All I knew was how excruciating the pain felt. Shocked from my own torture, it scared the shit out of me. I was sobering my reality, enabling myself to calm down. I thought, "What the f***k have I done?" I was barely calm, just calm enough to see the blood profusely running down my stomach and my legs. I'm scared, nervous, hurt, and exposed. I couldn't stop thinking, if I get caught in such a precarious situation by the kids, I'll be forever tainted. Humbly, I yell out to my fiancé. He angrily comes downstairs and sees me standing in the powder room doorway, covered in blood and becomes irate. Luckily, we lived down the block from the hospital and he insisted that I go or that he's calling the ambulance. I went.

Waiting in the patient room was bittersweet agony. Sweet because help was available and now, I'd be rescued. However, it was bitter because I didn't know what to expect. I was alone and I had to arrange a definitive story. I thought the best thing to do was to be straightforward and honest, I was enraged with my boyfriend. So, I did something erratic. I wasn't really trying to harm myself. It was just a cry for attention. I'm thinking, *this is no big deal. They'll understand.* Shortly after, a nurse came in. She didn't say much and barely made eye contact. She took my vitals, patched me up, and then excused herself. The next thing that I knew, I was being ushered upstairs, by an officer and another nurse to the psych ward. This was the longest walk that I had ever taken. It felt as if I were walking blindfolded, even though I wasn't. I had no idea of the final destination or who to trust because coming up here wasn't a part of my plan. Promptly, I started looking around and taking everything in. I was scared. The traditional hospital aroma of purified bacteria, menthol, and plain old plastic just compounded my physical angst.

Between the smell and the rambunctious butterflies doing somersaults in my stomach, I felt like I wanted to eject fluids from both ends. At this point, I needed to poop and throw up simultaneously. I didn't see any bathroom in near sight, nor did I ask because I refused to converse. So, my nauseating rumble gut travels continued.

The sound of beeping machines from all directions echoed and pierced my ears at every step. Amidst the odd stares from lethargic patients, I took as many mental notes of names and faces as I could. I neglected to chit chat with my hosts because I needed to be focused and alert at all times. I was clueless to just about everything that was transpiring. What I wasn't clueless to was my need for a quick defense. I was building my rationalization and justification for my actions, my case — with every step. The ward had a morbid temperament to it. The people were honestly frightening me. I uncrazied myself on that short-lived stroll. I, for sure, reaffirmed that I wasn't crazy, and I started to make a list of all of my good qualities in my head. While annoyingly saying to myself, *this is just great. They think that I'm crazy and they want to keep me here and lock me up.* I knew that I had to be on my best behavior from that moment moving forward. I was even offered meds. However, I refused. I didn't have the ability to freely roam around because I was being monitored. It was as if I was in jail and I needed authorization to call out. And, when I finally got the opportunity to, I called my mother.

She answered! That typically didn't happen. Her availability has always been sketchy and unpredictable. I gave her the intel and she was there in minutes. She also lived in close proximity to the hospital. Therefore, it was convenient for her. We made eye contact and her disposition looked like she was on and ready. As she made her way to me, I could see her wheels intensely turning. She was stern but looked puzzled. In my head,

I said, *Thank God!* My mother definitely grabbed her doctor hat on the way there because from the moment that she arrived she was speaking in their lingo. She's a doctor — a philosophical doctor to be exact. So, I knew I made the right call. I used my own wit and her jargon to get me released from being an inpatient at the psych ward. If the hospital had it their way, they would have kept me there for a nice and long stigmatized stay. Naively, I thought that I could just tell the doctors how stressed I was and that they would empathize. How sadly mistaken I was. It wasn't so cut and dry. I had to agree to depression medication and outpatient services in order to be able to leave.

Though I never complied and definitely should have, it was a huge learning experience for me. I learned that I needed to take life more seriously and to cherish and appreciate my liberty.

I returned home and nursed my wounds internally and externally. Months later, in 2002, while still living in the townhouse, I got up one spring morning around 7 am — as I usually did. I made oatmeal and wheat toast for breakfast, passed out vitamins and packed lunches. I strapped up the kids and pulled my Volvo out of the driveway to do the drop-offs. Styles was on a Ruff Ryder tour at the time and for the moment, the distance served us. Though it was more like single parenting in those days. I got back from the drop-offs within 15 minutes or less, since both schools were just that close. Although the usage of school buses would have been more convenient, I preferred to be their chauffeur until they got older, of course — which they hated, and my son still complains about. I fed my teacup York-ie, named Fifth Ave., turned the kettle on for tea, and proceed-ed upstairs to wake and bake; in other words, smoke. I gave my dad a morning call and as we were chatting, I started to smell smoke. It wasn't my kind of smoke. It was fire, material burning, smoke. I went to the top of the steps. The entire floor beneath was filled with smoke—black thick billowing smoke. I screamed to my dad, "I think I have a fire!" He said that he's leaving Brooklyn and coming to me. Styles was on tour. My mother was in Korea. There was no one else around. I panicked and called 911. I was able to crawl out of the front door, gag-ging with my night dress on, and ran to the front of the build-ing — jumping, praying, and crying. I never even had the time to grab my cell. After about the second jump, I realized that my dog and Tai's bird were both still in the house, but I couldn't go back in. It was impossible.

The firemen aggressively pulled up ready to roll. I told them that my dog was in the playpen that was located in the living room and if they could make a beeline straight to her. They immediately ran in, anxiously grabbing her, and bringing her out in a blanket. They did it so swiftly that they didn't even bat an eye. She was singed all over. It was heartbreaking. Unfor-tunately, the cockatoo had died. He was gone by the time they reached him. There was too much smoke inhalation. Luckily, the fireman said, Fifth Ave was able to turn and flip her body to keep the smoke and heat at bay, whereas the bird was too small. It was all too sad. We literally lost everything.

My father picked up my children from school and arrived shortly after. For Noah, who was still pretty young, it probably seemed exciting to him — the multiple fire trucks, with sirens and flashing lights. Perhaps, it was like a scene from one of his video games. Plus, he couldn't register the whole predicament in his little brain. However, my poor Tai, my little sidekick, was too coherent and all too aware! She was the one who was now growing with me. She was able to comprehend everything around her. She was devastated. I, wholeheartedly, believe that the trauma from going to school one morning and returning home to a deceased bird, birthed her extreme love for animals. It was a really distressing period for all of us. At first, we were so raw and frightened. However, God expedited support for us. Sometimes, you can experience something so bad that the harshness of it can be lessened just by the support you receive. It is almost as if the support is your pacifier. The love, kindness, and generosity of others helped me feel less consumed with the pessimistic aspect of things. And, that was the current state we were in. Thankfully, we acknowledged the outpour of support from our loved ones. Mike's sister drove up and helped me clean, tried to salvage some things, and even brought us goods. She brought necessities, some clothing, and toiletries. Though, Mike was nowhere to be found.

The fire had completely changed the vibe of living here. You can never forget a fire, especially one that destroys everything. The fire happening right after the new kitchen construction just added salt to the wound. I designed and then had installed a fabulous new kitchen — just for it to perish.

I was creatively stumped from the fire; it was such a major setback. If I were connected to myself more, at that time, I would have realized that I needed to produce more art. I needed to take the time out to paint and draw — something that I did when I was younger. I needed to do something that brought me so much joy and that I was so damn good at. However, my spirit wasn't calm enough to hear what I actually needed. Instead, I did what I actually wanted so that I could make money. I started catering and baking on the side as a hobby. I love to give, and I love to serve, especially good food because good food on a Tiffany's platter is love. The love in my food radiated so much that I was coerced to go professional. I started my own catering business. I was a one woman show with kids in tow, a move that revitalized my mood. I made everything from scratch — meticulous menus. Everything was traditionally made - all without a team. I catered to many magazines and video shoots and became known for my candied yams and peach cobbler, all thanks to G2's (my grandmother's) recipe. Later on, my famous red velvet cake would be the craze.

My world was turned upside down from the fire — and so were our pockets. Styles and I fixed up the townhouse, slapstick style, and put it on the market. We found a rental in Scarsdale and sold the townhouse in 2004 in White Plains, for $465,000. The real estate market was still lucrative then. Therefore, it was a great sale. Sellers were really cashing in. We relished in the sale — our first sale.

Getting back into the swing of things was productive and stagnant at the same time. It was a happy, but sad feeling. I loved the fact that I could start over by buying everything fresh. However, I was devastated and saddened by the loss of so much. So many mementos were destroyed. I saved anything that I could. There were so many custom features that I added to our home. All of them were destroyed. So, I was thoroughly frustrated when I had to abruptly choose somewhere new to live.

But I had to keep moving because my family depended on me. As we slowly adjusted to the new location, I was desperately in need of a night out and away from home. With my children under lock and keep of a babysitter, I headed into the city. However, the night came to a quick turn as I totaled my sister's Mazda that I borrowed for the evening. Canal Street was about a 40-45-minute drive from my house at the time. Although I got to my destination safely, my ride back would be a horrific nightmare. I have never been a heavy drinker — at all. I'll nurse one cocktail all night long. Most of the time, it was used as a diversion — I was deflecting conversation. I would just hold the glass to avoid or minimize being annoyed. I was trying to avoid the attitude of a gentleman who was offended because I replied truthfully by neglecting his offer to buy me a drink. But a simple, "No, thank you," is often misconstrued as confrontational.

Although I do drink on occasion, I still dislike the way alcohol tastes — no matter how much it's aged.

Nevertheless, on this particular night, I remember having just one Alize and feeling fine. I specifically remember being coherent and not getting behind the wheel tipsy. I was tired, yes, but not tipsy. Yet, somehow, I woke up on the shoulder, upside down in the car, about 100 feet away from my exit. I assume I was awoken by the slamming and flipping of the car. I gathered some composure and got my scruples together.

I finally realized what had just happened. I got out of the car and went around it, only to see that it was completely destroyed. It was all scratched up and the front was smashed in completely. I went back into the car and proceeded to try and start it. I got out of the car and I was now in shock because I almost died. Coincidentally, there was a live construction site on the opposite side of the highway. Clearly, they just witnessed this accident. How could they not have? The hugely lit fluorescent bulbs that they were using had me in the spotlight. Therefore, they saw my whole performance. Knowing that this was a bad look for a passerby as well as the police, I scrambled and scurried my ass off that exit. Following protocol, the police contacted the registrant, who was my sister, and then me. She didn't know what to say exactly, so she had them call me. In her defense, she didn't have any details. Plus, it caught her by total surprise, having to process the accident first and then her car being totaled second.

There was no legitimate explanation other than I hadn't eaten. Therefore, I was inebriated and tired. In turn, I misjudged the situation. Either way, I didn't confess. I didn't like the officer's arrogant questioning. So, all further questioning was discontinued. I know for a fact that the accident was a result of fatigue, the length of ride, a little alcohol, and a lot of stupid. But the accident wouldn't be the end.

My brother-in-law passed away and a few other dramatically incriminating incidents happened before fully moving out of the townhouse. Straightforwardly, I'd say that I've never encountered so much agony while living in one place in such a short time. Clearly, my mental state was unhealthy. I was twenty-five with two kids. That situation alone bares enough stress in itself. Thankfully, I persevered through this segment of my life. I survived even if no one can see my scars. My outer body appeared unscathed to most yet my insides were still wounded.

Most people are negligent to the fact that scars run deep and are buried under layers. It is sad that people prefer that you wear a T-shirt announcing all of your issues and scars — one by one, as if it legitimizes the amount of compassion that you are allowed to receive — like it is rationed. You don't know what anyone is going through. We are human. Therefore, be kind. Through all of the adversities that I have faced, no matter how strenuous, it has always pushed me to open other parts of myself to see what I am truly made of. So far, just maintaining a glow and being a light, something I take pride in, demonstrates that. Being an angry person in an angry world doesn't really take much energy. That job is easy. The challenge is to know, accept, and still live joyously. Still love thy neighbor and practice being the bigger person as much as possible. "Welp, my life sucks so now everyone else's will!" This statement is only said by miserable people. I chose to rise above and be a light. Smiling, loving and being compassionate, all take effort and is something that I still want to do and something I still want to portray. I smile because you're innocent to my strife and this is my journey. Plus, this is a strength and survival smile. That requires the kind of strength that you cannot see or understand. However, God understands. And, I believe that He prefers that I treat His people the way that He does — with love. It's easy to be angry and wear a frown and on those days, I retreat.

Often, scowling causes people that know you to assume that something is wrong — initiating conversation. They tend to feel the need to inquire and fix the issue — either that or they automatically write you off as mean or angry. I push through with a deliberate smile — a survival smile. Before, my smile was used as a mask to hide vulnerability. Now, my smile is used as a defensive, but peaceful mechanism. Essentially, I believe that God provides according to a potential mental, emotional, and physical endurance that only He knows you possess! He'll test you by serving heaping entrees of trials and tribulations. While he watches, you figure out what to tackle first. God is squirming from your angst all because He knows all too well that when you are done "playing with your food" (figuring it out), your dessert is a rich succulent and sweet medley of consciousness, self-love, and peace. I know that I shed a layer of skin those days just to taste the peace that I have now. But I can definitely say that it was worth it.

CHAPTER 7

Love at a Distance

David Styles was the breadwinner of the family and besides, he has been my shield and my primary protector in this life. He loves and appreciates me when I'm a crunchy hot mess in bonnets and soiled tees or when I'm in couture, strutting and sashaying the New York streets like a supermodel. If he wasn't spoiling and buying me something, he was loving me unconditionally. He really enjoys both. And, I guess I can say that I enjoy the benefits too. He has always loved out loud and is truly a stand-up guy. Styles is always teaching me something as well, be it about independence or love. He broadcasted our relationship from the very beginning and wanted my company over his boys any day. He's always provided everything, even if I was working. Whatever money that I contributed from catering went straight to the groceries, some utilities, and whatever shopping that I could splurge on. He's just different. This was another reason why I respected and admired him. He never micromanaged my funds. However, that was all over now due to the fire. Styles endured many sleepless nights to earn what so quickly got diminished. It truly broke my heart. The struggle for a black man to maintain and support a family, blindly, especially back then, was real. The odds were already against you when you had a certain upbringing. And, if you're demonstrating responsibility and consistency, as a black man, it is a threat to society. This was sad, but it was a reality back then.

We had no choice but to start over. What we accumulated thus far had cost so much. It was uncomfortable for me to talk about money, and even more uncomfortable that I couldn't contribute.

Therefore, my contribution would be being a good wife and mother although it was such a stressful time for both of us. He wasn't the healthiest or most stable person back then either — emotionally or mentally. So, we butt heads constantly; we had a lot of fights and disagreements. Some fights were more out of control than others — sprawling into the street. We were lacking understanding and compassion for each other. Our egos worked overtime because of our astrological signs. He's fire and I'm water. Therefore, butting heads can feel natural to us. However, he never wavered when it came to taking care of his family. We have always kept the love first.

Either way, having to start over after the fire was painful for him. It was painful for us. Styles not only had to manage hurdles at home but also in the music industry. Attempting to negotiate any morally or ethically correct business deals with the phony music industry is allowing yourself to be put through the wringer and enslaved. He wore those shackles for several years just so that his family could survive and eat. What do you think inspired the super hard rapping that he belted out back then? It was a combination of his past and his present. When a man doesn't think twice about selling one of his cars to get some bulk money fast, you know that he's a keeper. That was one of the many sacrifices along our journey that he made for us. His heart is bigger than anyone I know, which was one of the reasons that I was so attracted to him. His heart was just as wide open for Tai as it was for me and his son.

Upon moving to the rental in Scarsdale, I immediately got a cat. It was a gorgeous Siamese cat. This was one way to bring a new joy to the family after such traumatic times. We named him Miso. You know the song, "Black and Yellow," by Wiz Khalifa? Well, that is how we called Tai and Miso's name. We said, *Tai and Miso, Tai and Miso.* We did it because just like the song, those two were damn near conjoined. Wherever Tai was, Miso was, and vice versa. It was literally her cat. It reminded me of my bestie Blacky that I had. I'm referring to my pitbull that I had as a teenager. I had a bit of an obsession with that dog until he was let loose from our gate. I had such a special relationship with him. We all had a special relationship with him; he was like a human. So, I could identify with Tai finding a connection with Miso. This is when I saw how fanatical she was about animals. Having reflected on this previously, I believe that in my heart, this sudden love and passion came not only from losing the bird but out of her father's absence as well.

He was totally out of Tai's life at this point. Her aunt (his sister) was still in the picture, though inconsistently. I believe having pets was her idea of controlling the situation and making sure she received the love she wanted. It was like filling a void to a degree — something she could have to herself that would never leave. She would head out to the wooded area in the back and go digging and looking for insects or just about anything. She loved all things nature and connected through nature.

The kids went on regular trips to the Greenburgh Nature Center since it was directly across the street, along with the annual ice-skating group trips. Another aunt, my Styles sister, later took on my job as the children's new chaperone. That was one less outing for me and I thoroughly appreciated my me time. Tamisha, my sister-in-law, was always ripping and running with my kids. She's a big kid! She admittedly calls herself that. She was forced to go to the park with my kids about thirty-nine times a day as well. Before Tamisha began growing her own football team of seven kids, she would have endless time and energy happily exploring, toting my kids all over Westchester. The kids were busy and constructive, which meant that I was busy and constructive. They exhaustingly kept themselves occupied in the complex as well — frequently going to a small pool that was located at the rear of the property. Thank God for the recreational amenities they offered because for the next eight months, I would forcibly be the only parent in my children's lives.

In November 2003, Styles and I both had to "man up" *again.* He had to man up because he would be doing a bullet in Valhalla. I had to man up because I was alone with the kids. Not to mention, I had a lot of anxiety from the potential of him having extended time due to some altercation. To top it off, he was a felon already. Nonetheless, he was serving an eight-month sentence for an assault. I was beyond annoyed because the whole thing was inconveniencing, unnecessary, and avoidable. I was thrusted into single parenthood overnight. However, Styles did secure us with $17,000 prior to going away. I even had Gus, who was Styles' friend and like our brother, around and on-call as well. Since Styles' brother and father had passed away years earlier, Gus essentially fit the role of the male presence. Styles' main priority was having a male around for the kids and a helping hand around for me.

The absence of a father can have a profound negative effect on children. This is why Styles and I have always taken pride in reinforcing and honoring our beliefs of family first. Even though Styles was away, he communicated with the kids every single night and day. That contact took away some of the burden of him not being there, which gave the kids a sense of ease, comfort, and something to look forward to. Tai, however, had already experienced confusion with her father. So, it was extremely important to keep Styles in communication with her as much as possible and to have a male around. Styles may not have been her biological father, but he is Tai's Daddy. I think because he wasn't her biological father, his efforts amazed her more, causing her to always be perplexed by him. If her facial expression could talk, then some days it would say, "He's not obligated to love me, but he loves me so much!" Tai really looked up to Styles. You could see the glare in her eyes. So, if Mike was her first model for male love and it wasn't being expressed or delivered, then clearly, she was lacking in knowing what love was regarding her biological father.

This is why Styles was adamant about playing a healthy role in Tai's life. He lacked male support as a kid. However, he always tried to accommodate Tai, showing attentiveness in the best way that he knew how. Styles wanted to be all good in Tai's eyes. He knew that we've all heard, a *father is a daughter's first love* and what that statement significantly means. Although, if I'm being honest, the saying is a bit weird to me. However, I overstand it and get the symbolism behind it. My dad was my first love and treats me like a princess. I understand that bond and how vital that relationship is to my life. I love my father so much that I married him! Styles and my father basically share birthdays. They're a day apart from each other which means that the moment I left my dad's house, I essentially turned around and moved back in with him. It's no coincidence that Styles and my father are the most prideful men that I know of, which is another reason why Styles and I agreed not to bring the kids to visit him in jail. We didn't want any derogatory images to remain in their minds.

Thursday was the day that I went on my visits to Valhalla County jail. It was also where I went to subject myself to being treated as if I were a criminal. Every Thursday, my schedule consisted of mentally prepping, getting sharp, and picking up a girl named Leshawn to go to Valhalla. She was Styles' cellmate's girlfriend. Gratefully, she and I developed a genuine friendship during the course of this experience. Leshawn's loyalty and re-liability were what stood out to me. It was attractive how ef-fortless her support for anyone was. It never went unnoticed by me. She took her son on the ride to Valhalla to visit his father and no matter how uncomfortable she was with a two year old, she'd return bright and early next Thursday. During this time, I began working out not just for my body but for my mind. It was a way to keep me balanced and to increase my endorphins, something I did just for me.

One time, I remember smuggling weed inside the jail. This was for Styles' personal use. He was used to smoking every sin-gle day and I wanted to accommodate him. He didn't have to ask, insinuate or anything. I was just wired like that back then — proactive and instinctive, even for the not so good stuff. Badass! Since he was in a stressful environment, I was already ready, willing, and ignorant. I did that for all of the two times because I almost crapped myself the second time. Some badass I was, I had the weed balloons in my mouth because I had to transfer them through a kiss. I was sitting in the waiting room, impatiently waiting. Typically, you just sit silent and wait, make eye contact with your inmate and then proceed. One visit, I was silently waiting at my table minding my business, and an officer asked me something random. "Sh*t" was my first inner thought. The thought immediately registered sh*t in some other place too. The anxiety, from him standing so close, instantly triggered feelings of passing out, throwing up and diarrhea because I knew that I had to respond.

Therefore, I needed to discreetly shift the bags around full of saliva in my mouth, silently might I add, just to answer him. I did it almost gagging. Inconspicuously keeping the bag in a pocket between my gum and cheek, I forced the extra saliva back down my throat, and waited for my heart rate to drop. I needed to keep everything in my mouth, in my stomach, and settled. I proceeded and answered the officer — shortly my Styles entered, I made the transfer...and, all was clear. I told him, when he came out from the back, "Never again!" I told him when he came home as well! And he has never been back.

We checked jail off the list entirely. From then on, I was able to keep him more balanced with different perspectives on life. I made sure that he wouldn't incur any more charges. I helped by monitoring the places he went and monitoring who he kept as company. Unfortunately, when a rehabilitated violent black felon is trying to do better in life, he's actually prey — a target in this world. Therefore, some revisions in life had to be made.

PART II

CHAPTER 8

Sunny Way

We eventually bought and settled into our second home, located in upstate New York. 10 Sunny Way — a gorgeous red, four bedroom, four bathroom contemporary wooden home, greeted by a half-a-mile swirled heated driveway. The home opened to vaulted cathedral ceilings, a fireplace and a pool.

Our family's move upstate proved to be good for everyone, at first. In the suburbs, I was able to expand on the job of being a mother and wife. Even in rough times, motherhood is a role I cherish deeply, and I'd relish the kids' mementos. The act of deliberately standing, holding a lock of my children's hair from their first haircut along with preserved fallen teeth, is indescribable. The closest explanation for that feeling is like a baby's kick in the womb. I am enveloped by feelings of purpose and privilege when I hold them. Such feelings are the main reason I keep those remnants around especially after we'd lost everything in the fire.

As I delved further into the emotional tango that Tai and I had at the time, those same remnants often re-grounded me. From about six or seven years of age and on, I was able to see

Tai's personality bloom. Her passionate personality kicked right in. And, truthfully, it was kicking my butt. I was so busy with her that I often neglected Noah. When I say busy, I mean that I was kept on my toes. Tai wanted and needed more attention; and, that's why we're individuals! We are all different and require different things. Had I understood her more then, I would've insisted that she focused on pursuing her art. She was incredibly talented at such a young age. I, too, am an artist and displayed signs early on as a child. I would get in trouble for doodling and tagging anything. Instead of the negative reinforcement that I received for drawing everywhere, my parents honored and embraced their little developing artist by enrolling me into several programs. They bought me all sorts of easels; the shopping sprees on Canal Street for art supplies were major! But I was still a young-minded parent.

As Tai got older, I began researching places, eventually finding centers and clubs for her to attend. The whole process of researching information for a little human was all new and confusing to me! However, I was still trying to work with whatever awareness I had at that time. So, I placed Tai in several programs even though they were not always specifically tailored to art. I was still feeling my kids out at this age, Tai was fourteen and Noah was thirteen. I was figuring out their personalities the best way that I knew how — through trial and error (mostly error those days). However, both Noah and Tai were in programs. She loved gymnastics class, which was again, the same as me, and she took Taekwondo regularly too. Activities, activities, activities!

Tai and Noah also explored endlessly in our new home. When bored to no end, they utilized most of their time outdoors. There was a pond across from the house and depending upon the season or the moon, all sorts of things came crawling out of the water. Tai would be right there waiting to gather them and bring them into my damn house. Turtles fascinated her and without my consent or my knowledge, she'd sneak them into her room. She tended to them just before and after school, building a community of little makeshift homes for her reptiles. While cleaning one day, I stumbled upon the turtles. As she returned from school that day, I told her I'd found her secret pets but that it was fine to keep one, but that's it!

Just a few weeks later, Tai insisted on bringing in another turtle so the first would have company. It was hard to say no to that reasoning, however, my Styles advised Tai not to put both turtles in the same home given that they were introduced at separate times. When she didn't comply with nature's order, unfortunately, they both died. Their dead remains just sat there — for a long time at that. Tai's determination and loyalty to animals was apparent and she was devastated, to say the least. Even though she knew that her negligence was to blame, she was still puzzled and hurt. I still have the remains of her turtle and if you're calling me weird…welp, you're not very clever. His name is Vladimir. Vladimir was her four-legged friend during her grunge and goth days, hence the name. It's in the same family as Dracula to me, Transylvanian like. Tai got a bit discouraged with pets after that incident. However, those emotions were a blink in time because shortly after Vladimir's passing, our dog was pregnant three times within the year.. Tai sat and intensely waited during each delivery. Cautiously caring for each pup, she'd name them, bond with them, and claim them. I was glad to see her do so because with a 3000 square ft. home, two dogs already, two kids, about thirty-something puppies did not fit in my job description. I would think to myself, *well they're ok... their mother is there!* I didn't realize, again, that these were actual babies, with individual personalities. This was something that had already registered to Tai. Before and after school, she would religiously take care of the pups and the mom. She had a pure heart of gold.

Tai's sensitivity levels started to heighten. Mike was on a permanent sabbatical and living upstate was hard for Tai. I thought I was moving the kids to a nice suburban area where we could all bond with nature, have more space to roam, and access to better school districts. However, Tai struggled with her new location, it was too far from the friends she'd had before. As the children were still making the place home for themselves, David and I did the same and finally jumped the broom. Well, not physically. We decided to travel to Vegas such as many young couples and make our love official. Afterward, we had a large reception back home in New Rochelle decorated with $20,000 worth of flowers, something Styles just couldn't believe. Marriage made our unit stronger.

But not even marriage could help the kids feel more stable in their new home. After the excitement of the huge space, pool and nature died down, they were over it. Moving to Sunny Way completely conflicted with what my kids were used to. It was a total culture shock and it spiraled Tai into a depressive state on some days. Getting married and buying a house wasn't going to take away the fact that she was a minority — not in her class per se, but in the neighborhood. She longed for her father and still had a little brother in the mix. The uncomfortable transitions my kids were experienced gave me empathy for my own parents at that moment. I realized how making executive decisions for your family, even with great intentions, can pan out with bad results. I learned my kids may not see the lessons in that particular moment even though the messages were there.

Attending elementary and middle school on the Upper West Side, I know what it is to either feel like a minority or just be ostracized. In the '80s, everyone in Manhattan knew that most white people didn't go past 110th Street, which was where I lived — 112th Street and 7th Avenue to be exact (where I lived was on the cusp — so to speak). From the point of 110th and up, it was formerly all black and Latino, given that gentrification hadn't made its rounds yet. So, being young and black back then, you were automatically questioned by your white classmates if you stayed on the bus pass 110th street. The zip code change was enough to change the way that I was viewed though when I moved to Brooklyn, things were totally different. Those attitudes were clearly a Manhattan thing because Brooklyn was heavily populated with a melting pot of races. Therefore, you didn't know where anyone lived or was headed — let alone what ethnicity they were. Until then, I was in Harlem, where I'd travel on two buses to go to the *good neighborhood* so that I could attend school. To top it off, my parents put me in a gifted program called Columbus Academy. My mother said she did this so that I wouldn't get bored. She would say, "She's too smart. She needs to be challenged." However, the school had a segregated tone. Since I was one of the more colorfully behaved students, it seemed as if my colors would bleed onto the other pupils. This collateral damage caused me to stick out like a sore thumb. Days felt like months. I often wondered who was going to befriend me after seeing me in the principal's office and who was going to socialize with me at lunch because I chose to be myself rather than join a clique to achieve a certain social status. The days were draining because I was trying to keep up a facade of *I know that I live in Harlem and I'm dark-skinned, but I'm nice and clean.*

This was an artsy and eccentric program, with a very strict curriculum and great teachers. As a result, that building kicked out so many talented and successful people. Columbus Academy wasn't an all bad experience for me; it was just too lightly populated. In addition, I needed more diversity in an academic sense. You were considered bright if you attended Columbus Academy. I made a couple really good friends that I'm still in contact with today — like Emory and Mara! God privileged Emory and Mara with the grace of meeting Tai one summer as our bounds never fully dislodged. Columbus Academy gave me an understanding of how the world perceived a talented young black girl back then. They couldn't handle my young soul although they tried. I felt like I had too much going on at home. Therefore, it left me feeling as though I never took full advantage of the program. I know for a fact I didn't. I almost didn't graduate. When I got older, I appreciated the school experience there, but it was clear that I didn't see the message at the time. I didn't see the point or reason for me going all the way downtown to school. Luckily, my parents knew best.

Tai was now in a small town where everyone was familiar with each other. Trying to penetrate those unions and attempting to make friends was hard. They just wouldn't let her in. Tai was not walking, trotting, or jogging that extra mile to make or manufacture any relationship. It just wasn't happening. Plus, she had a brother and a cousin readily available. Tai was considered the out-of-towner. She was considered the odd one. It didn't make matters better that no one was ever able to make out her nationality. *Was she a Latina (Dominican or Puerto Rican)? Was she a Hindu (or someone just born in east India)? Was she just plain Asian and black?* These were just some of the breeds that they wanted to make her out to be. Perplexed by the ignorance, Tai would say, "I'm a person...first." I, too, have experienced this my entire life. "What are you?" They would ask with a distorted face because they've never seen a dark-skinned woman with certain features and her own real hair that isn't an afro. So, I would just calmly respond that I'm *a person.* Then, they realized they didn't get the answer they were looking for. So, they'd rephrase the question. Yes please, do rephrase that ish! *So glad that I'm more popular now.* Dark skin that is. I was a bit of an anomaly just up until a few years ago.

While I experienced much of what Tai was going through, too much time had passed and I'd forgotten just how hard it felt in the day-to-day. Had I remembered, I would have done things differently.

Another issue was Tai's father Mike. Although I didn't know the full scale of the effects that it had on her, I knew that something was off. I genuinely believe Mike was one of the culprits. Throughout the years, Mike's sister and I had a fallout. Therefore, our lines were cut. I had made a hasty executive decision and called CPS on her — a decision that double-backed later and bit my husband and I in the ass like a rabid pit. It was my first confirmation of how karma tasted. It is very real and it can regurgitate like acid reflux at any time. The decision was made due to me witnessing a few things that I declared to be unhealthy and unsafe for her kids.

This was something that I knew we couldn't have a dialogue about because she wouldn't be receptive. So, I wanted CPS to intervene. I wanted them to intervene as a wakeup call and for her to gain some tools — not to have her kids taken away by any means. Again, Mike has a huge family. So, it would have been virtually impossible for the kids to enter the system. I would have taken them in before that happened, especially considering the fact that one of them is my godchild. I was not too sure what the end result of the call was, but what I do know is that she was still the custodial parent and that the issue that triggered the call simmered down (I heard). *Was I wrong for calling? No. Would I do it again to someone else? Most likely not! Would I want someone to call them on me?* If I am harming my child, then, yes! Please and thank you!

Even though I sincerely apologized for any hurt that I caused, it still added a strain with Mike's side of the family. Feeling betrayed and hurt, she completely severed ties with Tai. Throughout it all, whenever I approached the situation, I always took responsibility and have stood by my decision to make the call. Whether or not anyone else sees the hand of God in it, I know why I did it and I believe that it *was* a wakeup call. However, due to this altercation, the communication was on ice. But the universe can attest that aunt Sharon and Mike have always had access to Tai. Even if they did not always have direct access, they did have indirect access as my dad still lived locally. My husband even took the time out of his preoccupied schedule to have non-deserving, endearing man-to-man talks with Mike repeatedly! Still, he wasn't fazed. There wasn't much else that we could have done. Even when given the perfect opportunity, Mike still neglected to do the right thing. We gave him her cell number, yet he fell short. What were we supposed to do? The ultimate mind-blower was that he had taken me to court for visitation rights two years prior, yet did not honor the court orders thoroughly.

He had his own version of acknowledging the order by paying child support inconsistently for one year. The stipulation was either $50 or $75 every two weeks— anything else that he gave was done at his convenience. Essentially, Styles and I did nothing because we couldn't. I couldn't force him to see Tai. As Tai got older, my husband and I could have gone to court too and played tit for tat. However, my butt was so overwhelmed with the court crap from before and I was tired of allowing the government to have personal insight into my household. I just didn't want to go through that experience again. Plus, let's just say that we were okay monetarily. So, I thought that it was a cheaper headache to just let him be. My sentiments were that I shouldn't have to chase Mike to be a father to Tai.

I could tell Tai was really feeling the loss of Mike and his family. She would randomly ask questions about them and act disinterested at the same time. Tai would genuinely inquire about her father prompting serious conversation and then abruptly stop and nonchalantly change the subject. I immediately picked up on that. I'm her mom and my instincts and senses are always tingling — sending off warnings and signals. My intuition and common sense tell me everything that I need to know in life. The last little bit of connection that Tai had with Mike was gone. From that point, Tai would see her aunt maybe two or three times when visiting her grandmother's house over a period of ten years. Two years down the road, I was forced to chase Mike to get in touch with him on behalf of Tai. I'd said that I wasn't barking up that tree again, but when it comes down to the wire, I'm unrelenting when it comes to my kids. So, if that meant extending back out, then reaching out again it was.

I'm a nurturer and a healer, also known as a fixer. It's been this way since I can remember. I tried my best to figure things out so that we could live as unbroken as possible. I wanted our family to be whole in every way. Remember, I was still a big ball of an emotional mess myself. I was constantly ticking, ticking, ticking like a time bomb.

I decided it was time for Tai and I both to attend counseling sessions. I was introduced to therapy as a young child, just as I was doing for Tai. I didn't have any other tools and simply did what I knew. Therefore, we went together. We had individual and joint sessions. I had to have therapy for my own issues, and I realized that I needed help with my anger. Tai needed help because she was acting out in school. In a nutshell, she needed help with her anger issues too. She wasn't fully aware of the behavior that she was exuding — she also wasn't aware of the connection that it had with her absentee father; though I was well aware.

My husband was on the road and we had this unnecessarily big house. It was a great luxury. However, I was ready to break free from my routine. I felt mentally enslaved. Emotionally, it seemed as though I was on a hamster wheel, running in the same spot, but going nowhere. I didn't want to attend another PTA meeting or pack another lunch bag.

Therefore, I figured it would be wise if I jumped back into baking to use my skills to produce edible art. I made the most dramatic, realistic, and deceiving custom cakes in Westchester. Before long, I was booked and busy, busy, busy! Positive encouragement, harassment, and intimidation were just a few of the tactics that my husband and sister used to get the entrepreneurial door open for me. I couldn't think past my kitchen, let alone going professional. After that inspirational battery was placed in my back, I was off.

My first major client was Manolo Blahnik. I thought that I would be starting small, locally, in the kids' schools. But no. I came right out of the gate with high priority clientele which gave me a new positive perspective on my life. I was busy turning my entertainment into a career.

Life began was good again, that is, until Tai emerged into being boy crazy. I made it very clear that I did not move all the way up here for this sh*t! Plus, I had daddy's voice in my head, *prudence* on the brain. I was trying to keep Tai appropriately dressed like a teenager and away from boys. It was daunting, especially due to how the other young ladies were dressed. Let's just say that their parents were more liberally lenient. Tai would change her look when she got to school, the same exact way that I did. She clearly inherited that genetic disposition from me; the only difference was I wasn't changing clothes. I was adding on loads of gold jewelry just to look ridiculous. I remember popping up to the school one day and shocked to see her coming out of class. We were both shocked. Tai was startled for obvious reasons. As for me, I was totally thrown off because I wasn't sure where she had gotten the tightest, shortest, mini skirt from. I don't agree with promiscuously dressed young ladies. So, it definitely wasn't something I purchased for her.

I finally compromised and allowed her to wear leggings. But even those were inappropriate to me. Leggings are just another layer of skin. In my head, it was the perfect article of clothing for a pervert or a Salvation Army Santa. Nevertheless, if I hadn't been so quick to assume and if I wasn't living in fear of Tai making the same mistakes as I did, I would have seen that most of her friendships with boys were platonic.

Everything gets put on hold once your teenagers start shifting hormonally. You never know the mood of the day — girls especially. With Tai now fourteen, I felt like I was physically squabbling with another version of myself on most days. My husband was baffled by Tai's moods too. His upbringing wasn't easy. So, he didn't have the tools to work with, other than his broken record mantra, "We will do whatever we have to." It was his favorite tune and always on repeat. Bless his heart, but he was also clueless. I would feel such pity for my husband because no matter how devoted he was to Tai, she wasn't satisfied. This man went above and beyond to make her feel special. He really obliged her. Ironically, she wasn't mean or even disrespectful to him, just to me! The fact that David couldn't fill her missing void was so damn frustrating at times. I would consult with my mom, but her answers weren't fitting for me. It was mainly because she had not raised teenagers. I would constantly have to remind myself of this. I also wasn't keen on taking her advice because she never met her own father. Therefore, she had daddy issues of her own lingering around. Hence, the arguments that we had were regarding my kids or parenting, which wasn't helping me or our mother-daughter relationship at all. I asked my sister, a single mom, but her little world was so perfect; she was really living the *Sex and The City* lifestyle with her kid on her hip as an accessory. My sister had no time for me and my niece, Asia, who was a baby queen with tiaras and the like, so we fought endlessly about my parenting style.

They weren't aware of all that I was going through at that time and vice-versa, but that didn't stop them from always being in my kids' lives while they were growing up. I really had to work to do it on my own with my husband on the road traveling for his music career. I was determined to get it right. No rock was left unturned for my baby. I paid the neurologist and holistic doctors because Tai was acting out in school. The neurologist was $500 a visit at Phelps Memorial. Although it was such a high price, we made a commitment to go twice a week for three weeks. And yet, every single exam or test that I put before Tai, she passed or was reviewed as fine and average. Though something just wasn't right emotionally. She couldn't get along with her peers sufficiently enough. It wasn't that she couldn't get along per se. It was just that things had to go more of her way in order for things to work smoothly. I didn't think much of that because I'm the same way. I've always been told that I'm special, as in highly intelligent. So, why wouldn't my baby become so as well? I now see and have learned through ridicule from family, that my standards are high and I'm a perfectionist.

Of course, I wanted my Tai to be perfect (in a subconscious sense, I guess). She's stunning. I wanted her inside and outside beauty to match.

Even though our surroundings upstate were bland, our family experienced good times hunting, sleighing, and BBQing at that house. Aside from the kids starting fires, my philandering husband, and the neighbor putting sh*t in the mailbox, it was a great place to live! Haaa! My house *was* amazing though. Terracotta floors, a cherry kitchen, vaulted ceilings, and skylights throughout. It was gorgeous! I just honestly couldn't stand that archaic town, as my sentiments began to match those of my children. I adored *my* house and my one neighbor Sandra. I also adored another black neighborhood household, the Artopes, whom my family and I befriended. The Artopes awoke to a cross burning on their lawn one morning. It was totally insane, and I began looking at options to vacate the little town.

My husband only associated with his weed dealer in the neighborhood. The local food options were McDonald's and pizza. And, to top it off, I located a trailer park in my community while I was jogging one day. It was appalling! We couldn't believe that we spent over half a million to be here just for a trailer park to sit in our backyard. We wanted out! We weren't discriminating but the residents from the trailers were all white. It was actually something that I never viewed in real life — only on television. I laugh at how my husband actually felt threatened by them due to how they were. Yes, my husband! He would say, "There's nothing worse than ghetto white people!" which always made me laugh.

Being from Westchester, he's seen white people from all walks of life. I'm from Brooklyn. Therefore, I was only familiar with prosperous white people that lived in the neighborhoods that my family couldn't afford. Therefore, I wasn't well educated. I began to predominantly stick close to home — essentially exercising every single day.

Bowflex, a 9-mile run, and a 3-mile inclined hill all became my pastimes. My body really responded well to living in the woods and running outdoors every single day. I trained as though I was in a competition. I would return home drenched yet elated because I was full of endorphins. I'd approach each day with a new goal, pushing myself to new limits. Slightly upset, but thoroughly mystified, my husband would say, "What exactly are you training for? Why are you going so hard and what's the point?" Time away from the city and living upstate allowed my soul to be touched by nature. The kids had genuine bonding time and my husband and I learned the dos and don'ts of reality. By living upstate, I was able to extract an appreciation for nature from my kids which was priceless to me. Even though I wanted out, I still appreciated the distance away from our friends and family. People had to consider a lot in order to drive that far and I loved that.

Ironically, my sister and the aunt's relationship still existed. However, Tai's and my relationship with her aunt was severed which is a real indication of how disconnected my family was and how polar opposites my sister and I are. Not only was this extremely uncomfortable for Tai and I, but it was also extremely bizarre to me. I couldn't quite figure out their incentives because my sister was involved with Tai, but neither her aunt nor Mike had the slightest interest. There was zero communication. Years went by with my sister and Tai's aunt in communication, however, Tai wasn't the focus. It was quite painful because as my child was hurting from confusion, so was I. When Tai witnessed my sister and aunt Sharon hanging out with their kids, who were her cousins, or read exchanges between them on social media, it was a shot to her gut. A few of her intriguing questions were: "Don't they know that I can see what's going on mommy? Are they purposely trying to hurt me?" It was painful. Tai was already hormonal. Therefore, this new layer of unnecessary drama had caused self-deprecating thoughts. She would painfully ask, "What's wrong with me?" and "Am I not good enough?" Those questions circulated through her mind. Since Tai wasn't emotionally prepared to endure such stress, it was crucial that I intervened. Within my capabilities, I knew that I had to peel back this layer of drama quickly. I refused to let this become her newest form of stress. Mommy gears were immediately shifted into hazard mode! Therefore, I asked my sister to reach out to her. Through her, I was able to get a hold of Mike. I was annoyed that I had to be in that predicament. But, respectfully, I humbled myself because it was my only vessel. I've always felt uneasy about my sister's relationship to Mike's family and how their priorities did not include Tai.

My ego straddled the fence. However, I have always done what my heart desired. I've also always done what was right for my kids. This was my last attempt to spark a connection between Tai and Mike. As Tai approached her more mature teenage years, she would soon be able to, and be responsible for, dealing with her father on her own — without my interference. I was frustrated because, at this point, I had given him her cell number and even my husband's number. I just wanted to be out of the picture. That way, there were no excuses, and no one could blame my attitude for his negligence. They connected. It was steady for a bit — longer than usual.

When Tai was eleven, I dropped her off at the Cheesecake Factory to meet him once. Tai said, gripping my hand super tight, "Mommy are you staying?" I replied with a smile, "Awww!" However, in my head, I said a resounding, "Hell no!" And thought, "We are just barely cordial, kid!" Another time, I remember picking her up from her grandmother's house in Brooklyn. She had gone out with him and his family. At this point, between the ages of fourteen to fifteen, she really started to see him regularly. Though things fell apart when I refused his girlfriend at the time from controlling all the comings and goings. I had no problem with another woman being involved with my child. However, I did have a problem with what I considered, a controlling woman, involved with my child. The girlfriend continued to incorporate herself in all things — events, plans, and quality father-daughter time. I felt too much pressure. At this point, she had a child from Mike as well so, I couldn't understand her or his actions regarding Tai. Mike and Tai needed to bond before having someone else navigate their relationship. They needed time to get to know each other, especially with Tai being thrown in the mix of their other children and family members.

Unfortunately, because I wouldn't agree to the girlfriend's dictating, we couldn't communicate, things fell apart and Tai suffered as a result. Although this time would be different because she was older and able to realize the effort from both sides during and after the disconnect.

Can you imagine how my daughter felt? She was dealing with not just his absence again but knowing that he now had other kids too. I wanted to aid her. I wanted to make sure that she was at her best all-around. I had been on a healthy diet path that seemed to be helping me feel better beyond the physical. I thought that it would be best to have Tai join me. It would at least move her concentration elsewhere. Changing my diet really helped with harnessing my thoughts and emotions. I was sure that it would do the same for Tai. After talking it over with Tai, I switched her diet and put her on various exercise programs. She was on a gluten free, yeast free, no dairy diet which aids inflammation, hyperactivity, brain fog, and so much more. Tai was cunning, to say the least. So, I had to stick to her like glue to monitor her diet. This way, I could get an accurate assessment to compare her mental, physical and emotional state before and after. I wanted to do all that was within my power to see my daughter well and happy. She fought me initially.

Though after seeing the benefits that came from her discipline, she later maintained the lifestyle.

Tai used her newly introduced tools, along with her art as a buffer for her life. She also began to play the guitar and write songs to express how she felt. During Tai's goth phase, which she lived and breathed, her lyrics became very unconventional, to say the least. Following the goth stage, she then went on to teeter between being a girly girl and a tomboy. She was an assortment of things, but it was still less than all that I encompassed. I was a dancehall, punk rocker, nerd, and African medallion wearer. That was Shabba Ranks mixed with Duran Duran/Madonna infused with Upper West Side sprinkled with some X Clan. Needless to say, we kept each other entertained.

Time at home with Tai was a complete joy. As she continued to express herself through her music and as she maintained a healthy lifestyle, my passionate Tai peeked out from under the bouts of sadness and frustration. I was elated and we spent much time together simply enjoying each other's company. Being at home was our thing as we enjoyed our cozy time by the fireplace. I can happily say that both of my kids are homebodies. I don't know why that makes me so happy. We baked, cooked, watched movies (mostly like Step Up), and painted together. Tai and I enjoyed Scrabble games, bike rides, and even long walks home from an impromptu hike — something that I am well-known for. If we weren't amongst, nature - God's art, cooking, or crafts, then most likely, I was counseling Tai regarding a jealous friend. Other girls were always in competition with her when all she wanted was companionship. We dealt with that a lot. Though over time, she did build a genuine friendship with one girl by the name of Abrasia. She seemed to be from a stable background which I really liked. Her and Tai became thick as thieves and Abrasia was a wonderful friend to Tai.

Tai was just like her mother in so many ways. I didn't even realize it before. It's so ironic how that happens. We, as parents, look at our children's behavior as isolated incidents, forgetting they're our kin. Along with finding a great female friend in Abrasia, Tai also began hanging out with boys often, over the girls. I reasoned that the boys were probably easier to hang around and she preferred their company, which was something that I felt and often did. However, I also believed Tai's affinity for her male friendships were tied to other areas of her life as well—the lack of Mike, the ability to control a situation (being a minority and a female), plus most guys always liked her (being flattered seemed to be soothing). While I understood, I would also try to deflect boy fever by any means. One great diversion, which inadvertently gave her a rewarding joy, was her pageantry.

Just before we moved, Tai had won several pageants. I'm from Brooklyn, we don't speak pageantry. I knew nothing about pageantries other than JonBenet Ramsey (may she rest in peace) and that memory wasn't pleasant. Therefore, my sister-in-law would so graciously take Tai to the American boy and girl pageants, which was great for me because it offered me much needed alone time. But, I wasn't completely off the hook.

I paid $600 for a dress, not knowing if Tai would win. I did it as a confidence booster. It was turquoise Taffeta blended with chiffon and tulle accented by cascading white and pink flowers with microbeads. The layers and layers of tulle seemed to bloom from under the chiffon, making the dress mirror that of Cinderella's. Tai entered. And, she won! She won for the most beautiful eyes which was no surprise. Tai's eyes are perfectly almond-shaped. They always looked drawn on her face. They were indeed synonymous with her beauty. Those eyes were something that boys loved, and the girls envied.

Oy vey, Tai was growing into herself.

CHAPTER 9

When Love Chooses You

"Myyyy Pleasure!" I can just hear Tai's voice in my head! As we moved our family to the Ritz-Carlton, she would mock the doorman. The way that she imitated them was a bit dragged out and freaking hilarious. It was a damn dream to live there and I was so glad to give that experience to my children for six years. At least my husband and I can say that Tai lived like a princess — sometimes Rapunzel! Our place was dramatically huge for an apartment. It was a three bedroom, four bathroom high rise in a full-service building. While I loved our home upstate, it was becoming a money pit. On the brink of the mortgage crisis, we tried to refinance, sell through a realtor, a for sale by owner — anything not to waste money. Yet, we completely got screwed settling on a short sale and lost over $300,000.

But the move turned out to be a worthy sacrifice. Tai made the honor roll upon entering the White Plains High School district. She was a popular girl for more than obvious reasons. Her dad was a famous celebrity. Tai was stunningly gorgeous and now she was on the honor roll.

"I have fans," she'd say returning home from school. It was a completely opposite end of the spectrum from me. I conspicuously had friends in high school, just not as abundant as Tai. I'm more of a quality over quantity type of girl and I need to observe you first. However, Tai is the more the merrier type of girl and once you've had a verbal exchange with her, you were sold on becoming an automatic friend or an associate. Tai had rekindled most relationships from our neighborhood from the home fire and now, they were circulating — something that I was so happy about. In White Plains, our children were also exposed to more culture which I'd longed for.

White Plains was a better experience for Tai overall. It was a good way to prevent her from acquiring certain stigmas, like the ones that stuck with me from the lack of diversity in my school. We adjusted as a family unit seamlessly. I was even working again in the building. I developed a high-quality clientele from selling baked goods. I lived where I worked, the money wasn't short and there was infinite love.

I became extremely busy immediately upon the move. I had quinceañeras, bar-mitzvahs, and just because clients almost every single day. I was thoroughly pleased with my work ethic. The money was self-rewarding. Therefore, I rewarded myself! Happily, I was making my own money so that I could feed my addiction, shopping! I would have the concierge conceal my packages until told otherwise. I would also make sure that he wouldn't give anything to my husband in case he should come home before I did. I wouldn't be a smart lady if I didn't take advantage of having white-glove service at the drop of a dime. Therefore, the packages needed to stay in rotation, which is probably why the residents and guests, alike, were always in awe of how we looked as a family — not because we were one of the two black families who lived there, but because we just added some flavor to the stiffness. We added Styles.

It's safe to say that we were a popular family there, especially Tai and I because everyone thought that we were sisters. Truth be told, we actually ran with it most days. We would chuckle like two kids amongst each other as we played it off, walking arm in arm. There were such good times. With Starbucks and Macy's across the street and my husband's NBA friends living in the opposite towers, it was just peachy. The Ritz Carlton is located in White Plains, smacked right in the middle of downtown, near malls, all the shops, and transportation - everything! Our corner store was the mall! When I finally loosened my grasp, allowing Tai more independence, she took full advantage of every shop because she wanted any opportunity to hang out. Therefore, she stayed employed so that she could control her adolescent time. Hence, this left room for her cunning ways. Tai was good at telling me that she had to work overtime when, in fact, she wasn't even working that day. Hanging out had become her newfound love — anything to have access to the streets. Sound familiar?

With new freedoms came new discoveries for Tai. She revealed one self-discovery to me and I was flabbergasted. In the spring of 2012, Tai expressed that she was attracted to girls.

Or did I read that snooping one day?! Not exactly sure. Either way, it needed to be out. Her sexuality was now on the table. This was the elephant in the room and, to be honest it was my worst nightmare. I was immediately taken back and standoff-ish. I wasn't sure how to femininely connect with Tai from that moment. I was just damn confused and honestly, really angry. *Why though? Was it because I didn't understand? Was it because I thought it was a fad?* Both were true. However, at the time, I just couldn't articulate it. The only thing that I could articulate was anger because I thought she was pursuing such relationships for attention. I felt as though she was doing it because it had become popular with her generation. It was trendy.

My husband is extremely confident in his being and comfortable amongst diverse crowds, so I'm not sure why I was surprised that he was more tolerant and understanding than I was. However, many might be surprised because if you know anything about the music industry that he's been associated with for over twenty years, it is ridden with homophobia. At one point, my husband was actually accused of being homophobic — due to some of his questionable lyrics. You see, early in his career, in the music industry, there was no real platform for open dialogue regarding homosexuality. There wasn't a playbook. Therefore, no one really knew what was considered acceptable or not. Homosexuality was shunned and minimally discussed even though it was blatantly obvious that some people were homosexual. However, with time came change. Besides, the artists who felt comfortable started to come out.

Homosexuality became more popular and mainstream — so much so that my husband even attended Pride in Miami with Tai and guess who stayed behind? Me! Honestly, I know my husband's love for Tai overrode any sentiments that he had regarding her sexuality. He would support anything regarding Tai. Nevertheless, he was in shock, but he took it like the G that he was. Me? Nah, I was mad!

Automatically, I began saying, "She better not try to come in here with her head shaved. I took it there right away. I wasn't prejudiced. I did have homosexual friends, but we never talked in depth about their sexuality or their sexual partners. We'd act regular and respect each other — with no weirdness. However, my friends aren't an extension of me. They're not my children and I don't have to worry about their well-being in that regard.

This uncomfortableness made me realize just how ignorant I was toward homosexuality. I wasn't just coming to terms with her sexual preference. I now had to come to terms with her being judged, discriminated, and worried about her overall safety. I went into a whirlwind of emotions. And, this went on for a while. It started to put distance in our relationship because I didn't know how to cope. I refused to have a dialogue about it. I wasn't going to be the virgin parent who exposed her daughter's bisexuality in our friend circle — that's for sure. I knew that curiosity amongst Tai's peer group was very prevalent, but I didn't have any personal references.

Therefore, I said nothing and acted as if it was going to obliterate on its own. I was a clear-cut example of blissful ignorance. Tai, however, was acting like a typical teenager and she just kept on being herself. It was obvious that I wasn't in acceptance with her sexuality and, because of that, we weren't meshing well together. Tai and I couldn't get the gumption to have a direct conversation about it. I wasn't mean per se. I was more antisocial because I felt like I didn't understand or really know her anymore.

Consequently, Tai's behavior started to change. She began acting out, running away, and skipping school. Tai was running around with the wrong kids. I saw the problematic behavior early on and Tai was way too stunning and talented to fall victim to the streets. Therefore, when my child is in need of guidance and I need intel, I become a detective or corrections officer. And, that's what I did. I ran a really tight shift. My answer to everything became, "No!" She would ask, "Mommy, can I...?" My automatic response was, "No!" This way, I could keep her as close to me as possible. And, in retrospect, I'm so glad that I did.

Tai became an asset to my business in the process. What, at first, was a chore, helping her mother bake and cater, turned into a solid job. It became a job that she was so proud of, so confident in, and was able to really display her organic talent. I was a self-taught cake decorator — aka a cake artist. I've done everything, from sculpting animals to hand-painting portraits. I had to do the most unimaginable painstaking work ever — it was very tedious and detailed work. Using cakes as canvases, it was labor that Tai and I both adored. Tai would spend hours, if not weeks, working on a special element for a cake.

Her talent surpassed mine, leaving me always inspired by her innovation. Now that she had become Rapunzel in the Ritz castle, Tai continuously read, wrote songs, and basically worked overtime with me if she wasn't in school. I ended up really relying on her. Therefore, when it came to giving out any type of discipline or if there was an issue, I had to tread lightly or else I was assed out! Tai would quit and completely leave me hanging teenager-style, totally irresponsible, with no care in the world. She did this on one or more than a few big occasions. The nerve of her! I literally would have to call my husband so that he could meditate, saying, "Okay, can you please speak to her because I won't, but I do need her help because she left me again!" I gave her 50% of every job. She would walk away with $200 to $400 per job sometimes. Yet, I had to kiss butt? So, I did...because I genuinely needed her.

Proudly, Tai would assure me that she could take over and plan for the future regarding my business. She always rooted me on to further the brand. Tai was the promotion princess, especially now that she had a solid and valued position. She kept a fresh stock of my business cards in her wallet and handed them out any chance that she could. Shocked, I saw my business cards in Starbucks once. That was Tai's doing and she even made sure that I was up on the bulletin boards in our building. I say this all the time: Tai is my #1 cheerleader and if she loved you, she was yours too. But what Tai wanted for me and others, she didn't necessarily want for herself.

Oddly, she lacked confidence in some areas, but blossomed in others. It's difficult being a temperamental hormonal young girl. I remember well. Most days, I was just in an unexplainable frenzy, not knowing that life would get better. Life gets better when you have more control over you! I can clearly remember the smallest issue seeming catastrophic to me. If my boyfriend didn't call me back within a certain period, that meant automatic rejection to me. Though it didn't mean that I was being rejected; it was just guys being guys. Tai, just like me, didn't get that the simplicity of feelings is just temporary and a part of growing pains. I wasn't as educated as I am now. I was in the introductory stage of becoming more conscious. I worked with the instruments that I knew best: my heart, my ears, and my motherly instincts. I wished, in those times, that Tai hadn't internalized things so much and shared more with me.

Tai would search for acceptance, often questioning herself as if she wasn't normal, or trying to fit everyone else's standards. This was something that I did at her age and something that I was partially to blame for. Admittedly, I'm a perfectionist with high standards and I am very health conscious. Hence, my lifestyle was too strict and intimidating for Tai sometimes. *Do as I say and not as I do* was the idiotic parental reference I used as law.

I was the boss and one should do as I say. This was something that Tai always rebelled against. I had to stand down many times from my kids because they don't back down. (They're really my kids!)

Due to their drills, I came to the realization that my style doesn't have to be everyone else's style in the family. That allowed me to be more lenient with my son moving forward. You honestly live and you learn if you pay attention. Nonetheless, health has always been a priority in our household — for example: eating right, mental stability, exercise — this was all of importance to us.

I'd hoped that being healthy physically, would help her maintain emotionally. Though, Tai still suffered. Mike's tie to Tai's insecurity issues were due to his exposure on social media. Tai had months and years of no communication from her father, no real mention, and no visit in sight. Tai would return home, go on a social media page, and randomly see him interacting with his other children and family members. Sadly, those unfavorable experiences caused her to question her existence. She would say, "What's wrong with me? How can he just go on and not include me in his life?" Those were a couple of inquiries she desperately had. Tai looked for Mike to validate her life and to validate his position in her life. She didn't want to speak or see him every three to four years and she definitely didn't want to see him frolicking with his kids on the internet. I believe that was the real beginning of the end of their relationship. I'd walk into Tai's room and see her crushed after having viewed happy images of a father she didn't know as such. I had to clean up the chaos. After the social media revelation, her interest in him and his side of the family appeared to have lessened. When she did actually seem interested, his family and the lack of her being involved was always at the peak of questioning.

Interestingly, we all have questioned ourselves at one point or another in terms of being valuable. Haven't we? I know that I still have many doubts as an adult. I only live up to my standards now though due to growth. But, for the people who don't, you have to stop! You must live for yourself. You can't live for your mother, father, sister, brother, child, or friend. You can't provide your best when you're not whole yourself.

Tai began living for herself as much as she could, along with me by her side for supplemental support. She tried her hardest to fight the feelings of neglect. I could tell. She'd show solid months of strength and resistance. However, there were times when she'd go on Facebook or Instagram one day, perhaps during mercury retrograde, and she would become completely reclusive. It was obvious to me, not so much to others. She'd try to save face, smile, and prop up when I came around, hinting to the fact that she was all great. I always saw past that smile or past that random come lay in my bed up underneath me thing she did. That's why I often suggested that we go to the art supply store or for a jog to clear our minds. Perhaps, we would watch Sweeney Todd, Step Up, or Disturbia; an intervention of her favorite movies.

Tai weaned away from Mike and the older she got, she just stopped mentioning him and his family altogether. I believe my daughter was ready to move on and disconnect completely. She was now fourteen and therefore, she comprehended everything herself — not by a mother to misinterpret or get anything lost in translation. Tai was her own witness. Either way, she knew that I wanted to help ease her pain and see her smile. So, she withdrew indulging in her father for a while. This is when the internalizing began.

As the years moved on and Tai neared sixteen and seventeen, there was no longer a will to express organic emotion when it came to her father. I felt as though I was pulling teeth to get her to even focus on him. She was thoroughly into women now. So, a deadbeat dad was definitely not on her list of favorites. When I'd assume something was wrong or just bring up the other side of her family, she only had two responses, "I really don't care about them" or "I just don't understand." "I really don't care," meant she actually cared but was neglecting to show it. "I don't understand" was said because she really didn't understand dammit and neither did anyone. I've always felt uncomfortable knowing that those were her feelings. Her emotions toward her father and his family was something that I could never remedy. Therefore, when it came to dating in the future, I just let her have her experiences. I wanted her to find joy and peace.

At times, Tai dated guys and girls. And, ultimately, she seemed happy. She was always out or working with me; that was flowing well. Her cell phone was its own entity. It truly had a life of its own. A cell phone is a magical place for an imaginative teen. Due to such heavy communication, she always had big things planned. She had a hike here, a party there, or even ended up in Brooklyn getting a tattoo. Tai was an explorer — your average teenager! I always told her that I admired her, being bisexual, having options and that it must be kind of fun. Maybe if I were able to stomach the kitty, perhaps I would have experimented too!

I made a 360° change in terms of acceptance of Tai's lifestyle — as if anyone should be waiting for acceptance. You will never truly know the evolution of my feelings from how they started versus where they are now. I went from not having one single solitary direct discussion about it with her to shopping for dildos (not at sixteen or seventeen but when she got older). My epiphany came from a random conversation that Tai and I were having one day. We were walking in the city vintage store. Thrifting was a thing that we did; we were strolling and casually talking per usual. I can't remember who said what first. But I remember asking her at one point, "But, how can you not know what sex you like?" I spoke with such random directness that it would always make people uncomfortable. I asked because we were shopping and in terms of styles, I wasn't exactly sure what to offer her. So, I went in with questions. She turned her head, like the exorcist, looked at me, and said with slight frustration, "Mommy...I just like people. I'm not looking for either male or female. I look for vibes and connections. That's what is attractive to me." It made a world of sense.

Tai eventually brought someone home to meet us. The only significant long-lasting relationship that Tai had was with her bestie A. A is a sweet tender soul, who is the most responsible and most parent-loving youngster I know. She is an attractive Latina and very respectful of my husband and I. When A and my daughter started dating, Tai was eighteen. Strangely, A was adopted and had no real connection with her biological father who also lived in Brooklyn. Even more coincidental, her father's name was the same as Tai's father. I thought, God really is comical with his irony and acknowledged the synergy.

I think both Tai and A needed their own kind of love. A love that they could control and manipulate. There were some serious synchronizations to detect. There are no coincidences, it's all a part of the plan and your journey. Tai and A were going heavy from 2013 to 2015. It was heart-warming to witness. Tai was being courted and getting all the attention that she wanted. The two went everywhere together and they were just two youngsters growing up alongside one another. It was really sweet, innocent, and healthy. I was in total support of their relationship. Tai and A really cared for each other; it reminded me of when my husband and I first got together. I could feel that it was genuine.

We had some really good wholesome family time in the Ritz along with having hosted some fabulous parties. I'm truly thankful to God for it all. However, the huge life-changing blessing that came from living at the Ritz was priceless! It was a profound change to my life: a gift of mental clarity. It was an overall bodily flush — a toxin cleanse! It sounds so basic and simple, however, it's not. With my family starting to feel grounded, it was time to focus on myself. I didn't know that I needed such a mental purge until God forced me to see it, as He forces me to see everything.

I suffered from Candida. Candida is an overgrowth of yeast in your bloodstream. I contracted the infection either by a diet high in refined sugars or antibiotic use. Birth control pills are culprits as well; however, I've never taken those. Birth control pills seemed way too inorganic for me to tamper with. Plus, the whole concept just never sat still with me. Escalated Candida symptoms are major stress, fatigue, brain fog, arthritis, inflammation, ulcers, and food sensitivities along with a whole host of other shit. I literally woke up one day and was allergic to my favorite foods, I couldn't walk from arthritis, and I had a mouth full of ulcers. I do not wish this pain on anyone. And, to think that I believed I was the healthiest person alive! I mean I was on 6 oz. a day of wheatgrass! For this to happen seemed absurd! So, when I became ill, I was in complete shock. I was even more appalled when three different doctors misdiagnosed me and had me under the assumption that I had an autoimmune disease called, Behcet's. There's something called common sense and knowing about one's personal body. I'm pretty smart. So, I figured that I had to do as much research as possible until it made sense. And, with collaborated efforts, it did. My mother ended up diagnosing me.

The healing process began, and light was ushered in immediately. The illumination brightened up my entire reality, giving me a clear precise outlook. However, before savoring such euphoria, the transition was absolutely horrendous for me. I went through it but survived as usual. The detoxification took about three months in its entirety. It was a tedious and extremely painful process to go through that I will never forget. Insomnia, rapid weight loss, and excessive sweating along with painful ulcers topped with arthritis. It was a terrible time! I was hostile and horrible company to be around. The origin, detox, and the maintenance of Candida was something that I vehemently studied. Now that I'm so versed in Candida, I can monitor myself and my diet to prevent it from happening again. So far, I'm good! I could clearly see the difference between my thoughts prior to my cleanse and after my cleanse. If one doesn't have any kind of clarity, open-mindedness, peacefulness or just some kind of enlightenment post cleanse, then, my friend, you've done something wrong!

It was the best and the worst time of my life. When you're in that much pain from detoxing with ulcers, all you can say to yourself is that this pain must be worth it in order to expel harmful toxins from the body. It was a crippling and heart-wrenching pain, all from detoxing. I emerged a new woman, a new me. Thank you, God, for that forced halt! That transformation set the tone for the future. Now fully cognizant, I'm able to gauge my mental status and maintain some clarity. My diet was forever changed for the better and the family diet was also forever changed for the better. No refined sugars or starches made it into my home. Therefore, I felt like a drug pusher when I had to make cakes for clients. I loathed buying that junk. White refined sugar is pure evil: a real silent killer drug.

In between this time, another set of life-changing unfortunate events took place. Another painful hurdle was approaching, and it was coming so fast that I couldn't even brace for it. "Can I get a minute, God?" I begged.

Tai acted out one holiday weekend. She ran away. She's done that before. Sometimes, just to Starbucks for a few hours and back home or even to a friend's house overnight. This particular time was different. Not only did she run away, but this time, it was a whole production. Tai used her teenage powers to manipulate a situation to her advantage. It was an example of her cunning ways.

Tai approached her biological father's side of the family randomly via social media. She had side talks with them unbeknownst to us. Tai went on telling lies and expressing all sorts of unnecessary things to them about my husband and I. That's not the shocker! She was acting as a hormonal teenage girl that I wouldn't allow to have sex in my house, smoke or drink, or come in at all hours of the night. Therefore, running away was no surprise. The shocking part was the adults who were involved. They knew me very well, but believed her. It was extremely hard to process that these adults were buying into what Tai sold them.

Nonetheless, someone was looking to cash in. So, they did. The adults never, not once, contacted us, her actual custodial parents. They contacted the authorities and you can imagine where it went from there. CPS arrived within four days. However, it worked out for my family because my caseworker was able to see through and smell the BS within an hour of being in my high-rise. Nonetheless, Tai was staying with family members through the duration of the drama.

Good for her because in order to not escalate the situation and to save my sanity, I most likely would have asked her to leave anyway. I actually thanked the betrayal of the adults involved and Tai too — not for betraying me, but for thrusting me into a growth spurt. She was used as a tool for me, for them, and for herself.

This is a very important piece of history, Tai's history. This situation really weighed on her because she couldn't necessarily articulate that the action was a cry for help. She couldn't express how she really was angry from the past, but still, willing and wholeheartedly, (contrary to what it had seemed), wanted to be involved with them. But I knew it.

Those circumstances changed me even more for the better, forcing me to find even more strength. Yet, this Olympic-style hurdle had proved differently. I was restored with some kind of other strength — a kind of bionic strength. Thankfully and ironically, God had just given me that new layer of defense to use. I had just cleared my body of unhealthy foods and substances. Therefore, my mind was alert, my perception was keen, and I was super sharp. My strategy for approaching adversity was now different.

Tai, perhaps, thought that it would bring her closer to her father's side. However, it did just the opposite! She felt responsible and felt as though she could never rectify her wrongs. I forgave her instantly, not just because I'm her mother and believe in unconditional love, but because I knew that it was a cry for attention. At this point, any bit of attention from Mike's side, be it good or bad, she welcomed. Plus, she was only seventeen. She was clueless, but she wanted to salvage whatever relations she could. I insisted that Tai apologize. So, she did. She sent out a group message that she composed all on her own. Tai apologized sincerely for her contributions.

Ignorantly, she only received one acknowledgement from that apology. Just one out of the three adults, who partook in the mess, was able to love unconditionally and do the honorable thing. This was truly heartbreaking to Tai. This person was the only one to acknowledge my hurt and their misjudgments as well. I sincerely needed that for my own personal sanity. I know my relationship with God and that he knew the truth. I let it play out. Tai and I were good and that's all I cared about. Thankfully, she willingly acknowledged her participation in the debacle. This was a great incentive for us to move forward. All Tai repeatedly said was, "I was seventeen and they were the adults." And, I agreed.

The thing is when people have personal issues or hidden agendas, they can sometimes project that on you, your kids, your husband and your family. They use other people as pawns in their game. Yes, it's possible. I believe that God used these people, at that time, for certain reasons. And, had I not been on the righteous path already, I would have diligently got in everybody's ass! If it weren't for the guidance, love, and protection from my husband, I definitely would not have had that discipline!

During the five months that Tai was gone, she experienced a few things which allowed her to make her own judgements regarding Mike's side of the family. I mean, in all honesty, the whole situation was built on a lie. How was it ever going to end well? Tai, too, had to learn that. But Tai just wanted to be done with the whole situation. I sat back and let God do His thing because the truth always surfaces. This situation didn't matter anymore to me because my baby was fine and back home with me!

This incident changed my relationship with Tai for good, for the best. Prior to this, I was still giving Tai a manufactured perception of myself. I had always been afraid to be 100% authentic with my children in fear of them making the wrong choices in life. I was fearful of them judging me as a parent rather than a human. It was sheltering to a degree — not allowing certain music to be played, them not knowing about my smoking habit and certain friends in my life. I was just trying to make life seem not so real. This backfired when Tai became a teen because now she was exposed to the real world. And, with that, came more challenges than expected because some things were shocking, especially the way her generation and peers conducted themselves with their parents. Sheesh, so difficult! They were like adults from thirteen years of age. This was something I didn't agree with. But, by the time Tai returned, I said screw it! She was going to see the good, the bad, and the ugly side of me — in a loving way!

Seriously, at thirty-seven, I had literally just started being human and myself. I was very transparent at this point, which actually brought us closer and allowed her to make her own real assessments about me and her life. There was no more pretending! It was just the real me. Having realized that I was really dealing with myself all over again, I started accepting her for who she is…because she is me!

CHAPTER 10

And Sometimes We Must Let Go To Hold On

A matriarch is a gift that life gives you if you're lucky — and so is a grandmother. G2, which stands for grandma 2 (like T2 for Terminator 2), was my grandma. Betty Irene Grice aka BIG, was my first "Big"! Notorious B.I.G. (Biggie Smalls) was my second. She was the family's foundation. She was my shero and I'm so thankful for her. It seemed as though the baton had been passed on to me since her crossover in 2014. It was as if I was the new matriarch, with responsibility or duty to keep the love pumping in our veins — just like she did. It's beyond difficult though, I must admit. It's hard to keep contradicting personalities, perspectives, and egos sticking together once the glue is gone. She was our glue and she was like Gorilla Glue. Before I can even begin to fill her Chinese moccasins, God took me through some real trenches and valleys. I wasn't sure, and I'm still not sure if I'll ever fully exemplify her strength. However, God keeps showing me that I'm a contender.

The lease was up at the Ritz and my husband, and I decided against paying over $5,000 in rent to stay. We had to make wiser decisions and better investments. Tai had graduated high school and we were trying to figure out her next move. Noah was a sophomore and he was eating everything. So, we were trying to figure out his next move too! He was really growing by the hour before he went plant-based at sixteen. This was impressive and incredible, which is indicative of Noah's unique personality. My husband and I didn't want to alter our lifestyles so we were just trying to figure out what was a good plan all around. The best thing we could come up with was to sacrifice. We thought it was best to temporarily separate as a family and we would purchase another property in about a year. In the meantime, we'd save and research properties elsewhere, prioritize some things all at our leisure — with no pressure. So, I went to Sarasota to get a beautiful place in the same vicinity as my mother's home.

Tai and I moved down South. I was an adult although clearly, the little girl that was chasing mommy still lived within me! My maternal grandmother had just passed away and my mother was grieving alone in Florida. I felt compelled to go and spend time with her. It was a mixture of me wanting to comfort mom mixed with tidbits of the little girl lost syndrome I still had. I was still kind of chasing her to a degree since childhood. I wanted to take advantage of that time to finally and genuinely bond as adult women together — with open, honest, and healthy dialogue. I wanted some real truths. The only problem with that was that I had expectations. Expectations are beliefs that something will happen, but it doesn't mean that it will. I also wanted to reminisce and just shoot the breeze about my grandmother. Who would be better to do it with than her own daughter? It was hard to believe that I wouldn't be making any more trips to the Harlem River houses, where I would see her in the midst of a Rucker's tournament or before a Grant's Tomb Night or coming from the famous fish market. She's taught us all so much — so much black culture, gems, and survival to be exact.

G2 introduced me to Pan, Pan's Breakfast, Flash Inn — a local spot where the throwback gangsters frequented and a few others. It is unfortunate that most of the famous eateries in Harlem are now closed but thank God for G2 because I was able to patronize the great ones! Harlem, the diamond in the rough amidst the crack houses, was like its own little planet with a plethora of authentic ethnic flavors — like the Indian Bombay restaurant that was on 125th and Amsterdam Avenue, which served an exquisite coconut soup — the most flavorful meals all served on their original tableware. I was obsessed with bean pies and the halal pizza in the Muslim community as well as these amazingly hot and fresh cinnamon rolls from a Jamaican bakery. It amazed me how they always gave me extra icing. It was as if they could decipher what I wanted by the glare in my eyes. And they were right, I certainly wanted more. However, the potential of being perceived as an ungrateful kid just didn't seem like it would be fun. Therefore, I knew to dare not ask.

I've always enjoyed a good meal. However, having learned that not all good meals enjoy me, I eat clean.

Nonetheless, the Harlem experiences with G2 were amazing and thoroughly educational! G2 even introduced me to the five-finger discount, which has seriously been a tool that I have appreciated and learned a lot from. Boosting and stealing in my young days taught me intuition, camaraderie, the laws of life, techniques to survive — things that Seward park could never do. Okay, so maybe that wasn't amazing, but it was educational! It has helped me to survive — gotta love her!

G2 was a feisty, straight shooter with an enormous heart. She's another proud Sagittarius that I've been molded by who grew up in the Depression era. This made her awareness and tolerance much different. She hated the direction that the economy was going in. I literally had to refrain from telling her how much my mortgage was in fear that she would break out in hives. She just couldn't wrap her head around certain prices. She was a gorgeous woman, headstrong, street smart, intellectual, with a Native American flair, all wrapped in 5ft. That was G2 — muscled and strong! You never knew her age nor did she ever tell. And, if you did ask her, she would most likely say, "You've got some unmitigated gall."

I love G2 and to watch her gradually fade was very tough to endure. This was extremely hard for our family. Even though she was 92, no one is ever really prepared for death. Plus, in my mind, strong people just never get sick or old. It was a hard visualization for me to see a physically or mentally strong person get vulnerable and weak. It was even harder for me to accept it as reality. However, it was time, so I was forced to embrace it. My other grandmother just turned 100 and I only knew one of my grandfathers — who also made it up there. Therefore, G2 was my and our immediate family's first real blow. I couldn't believe the aerobics instructor who lived in the YMCA wouldn't be there anymore. Where was I going to get my style influence from? G2 had amazingly effortless style — a little under-aged dressing mixed with '70s chic, with a little roaring '20s, plus a Kufi. That was G2! She was such a rockstar. *Who was going to give it to me straight? Who was going to give it to my sister straight? My mother straight? Who was going to keep us all in check now?*

I thought it was best to temporarily stay down in Sarasota — allowing my mom and I to heal together. It would also give Tai time to get her priorities in order such as a license, career options, and so forth. I could also finish my first book on relationships that I was writing at the time. Plus, the flight back to New York was only three hours and I could get away for a bit. The boys could come visit at any time.

At this point, my marriage was dead solid. So, I honestly had no issues regarding a temporary change — and that's just what we did. Hubby, Tai, Prince (our maltipoo), and I drove down to Florida. I was extremely grateful to have that opportunity. I love the warmth and seeing the actual sun, but the real perks were being able to have a break from dusty and dark New York. I couldn't think and write there. I love New York, but it can be depressing at times.

I also really got to bond with my sister/daughter. It was a true blessing. This was the time that Tai and I became closer than ever before. There were no visitors or distractions, just time for me and my girls.

For the next seven months, Tai and I were pretty much tethered together! To the point where I purposely would not turn on my television some mornings to imply that I was still asleep — basically indicating, not now! She had me all to herself and she loved it. Tai had a chef, a baker, a nutritionist, and a personal trainer all at her luxury. And, might I add a therapist? I barely took that hat off because she was maintaining a long-distance relationship with A. Therefore, I had to somewhat supervise the relationship's twist and turns. We got our Tragus pierced together — an extremely painful piercing. We did no research and had no basic understanding of what we were getting ourselves into — essentially, we just signed up for some suffering. Overzealously, I went first and took it like a champ! It was painful, but I acted unfazed. Therefore, Tai thought that it was a breeze. When it was her time, they had to stop in the middle of the procedure because Tai was having convulsions, "Seriously mommy! You couldn't say how painful this was?" I still laugh about it, seeing her face and hearing her voice. We had optimal time with each other.

When I say that we talked and expressed a lot, I mean exactly that. We shared so much about everything — from my personal struggles to us molding her future. We had sincere, genuine, honest, and candid talks. It was so refreshing! I was glad to gift this to her and to show her my vulnerability as a mom and as a human. I shared things with Tai that I never thought I would previously — the unmasking was a feeling of relief. I lived in gratitude for all of the positive moments. Though she, of course, did annoy me, it was a different kind of annoyance. It was something I was able to cope with and tolerate — an annoyance that somehow allowed me to fall back and let her learn from her own mistakes. Perhaps, I was just letting go a bit or being more trusting. Or maybe I simply had less stress because I had one kid with me instead of two? I don't know the exact answer. But what I do know is that it just felt good to see her in control of her life instead of me being in control of it.

With less pressure, more conversations flowed. Tai was more willing to admit to her wrongdoings whenever we had an issue. I appreciated and I acknowledged it. I was basically feeling comfortable with the woman that she was becoming. I was proud. It was so amazing to watch. I was really seeing the fruits of my labor. In my head, I would often say, "Look at what God and I created." I would literally thank God for allowing us to have peace with each other because there wasn't anyone around for her to run away to.

Our diets and bodies were at their best. We had schedules of working out and eating clean daily. Tai reaped all the benefits. She was leaner, her hair was growing faster (all she cared about but wouldn't stop flat ironing or cutting it). Tai's skin was clearer, and she had a vast amount of energy that kept inclining. She was disciplined enough to take her vitamins, walk to work at our local Walmart and not go ballistic on the coworker that either nabbed or nixed her lunch. If you knew Tai, you knew that tampering with her personal food is her Achilles. You're basically a dead person. She doesn't play about her food.

When the incident took place and she came home and calmly articulated what happened as opposed to the security office calling to tell me that they're holding my daughter, I was shocked.

This was when I saw the benefits of clean eating, exercising, and having minimal stress. My erratic, negative, and impulsive responses totally left, and I was glad to see Tai's being removed as well. This was right in time for her twentieth birthday that was coming up and since her girlfriend was coming to visit, Tai wanted to have herself completely together.

We had been living there since October 2014. It was now March when Tai randomly approached me, per usual, one day and said, "Yeah, so…I'm gonna get my own place with my girl-friend." Now, it was time for my exorcism moment. "Umm… excuse me?! You're going to what? When? In another state? With whom?! Wait what?" Basically, I had served my purpose to her already. Tai had no more use for me and thought that there was no need for me to be underneath her, smothering her but - so she thought. I got her on the road to responsibility and now she's ready to just up and leave. Initially, I should have been happy. However, all I thought was how a thirty-day notice was not enough time to process this news. My answer was no. "

Happiness wasn't my first sentiment. I loved the thought of her new perspective on life for the both of us. But, perhaps, sometime in the near future. Besides the fact that we just moved here, I wasn't ready right now and she wasn't the most responsible either. My husband and I spent a lot of money and exhausted a lot of time and energy to move down there. Moving is not how it used to be. It's a really expensive business, especially moving out of state. Nevertheless, Miss Tai didn't care. Although she politely asked, she already had her mind wrapped up in a bow. She was ready. So, I felt completely bamboozled about her flick of the wind thought. The honest truth was that under all of the fear and nervousness, the real terror lived. The fact of the matter was that I never wanted her to leave me. I never wanted her to move out. Whereas most parents wanted their kids out of the house, I wanted them to stay in my home forever. I've actually told them that. I knew that wasn't an option though. I knew that it would eventually happen, but I just didn't know that it would happen so quickly. So, my initial reactions were a bit overdramatized, in hopes of manipulation or persuasion of some sort. I'd ask, "Are you sure (with the 'r' enunciated)? Is this what you want? Have you really thought about this?" When those didn't work, I also asked, "Tai, maybe you need more therapy before moving in with someone because relationships change when you live together." That didn't work either. I even threw in another thought by saying, "So, you do know that your family is three hours away by plane and you'll be alone and when you have an argument or disagreement, you can't run to me? And, when you need to borrow something, I won't be there. And, when you want me to train you regarding working out, I won't be there. And when and when and if and if." I literally pulled anything to get her to change her mind...no cigar! She wouldn't budge. Her mind was made up.

I had thirty days to get myself together. How nice! I even thought about staying during the transition period just to be close, but that meant that my husband and I would be paying three rents, which was not frugal. It was why I was so annoyed with her leaving in the first place. Actually, I was more than annoyed. I was very angry, which resulted in tension between us. I was cordial, but I didn't really engage for two days. I just felt so unappreciated for the lack of communication and sad that she was finally leaving. Unwillingly, I had to understand that it was what she really wanted to do although her approach was off-putting. It was so easy for her to say what she was doing. Kids these days have no awareness of what a real struggle is. So, all of the advantages and support that they receive is natural to them as if they're supposed to have it. Because, if Tai really, really knew the struggle, she might not be sprinting out of the house. She was more responsible than me at that age because clearly, I was desperate to leave home. Kid and all, my ass was still at daddy's house until my husband's influence kicked in. I was so angry with Tai that I actually had to have conversations with my mom, dad, and girlfriends regarding this. I was looking for anyone to support my feelings of her not being ready. All the while, I was pondering if this was really my reality and I was petrified. I remember it was as if I knew something was going to happen. However, the worst was never a focus, fragment, or option in my mind.

Nonetheless, because of the conversations with my loved ones, a lightbulb came on, which is why I like to talk to several people about the same subject so that I could get mixed opinions. Sometimes, they aren't mixed at all and, in that case, I focus on the messages that come from the majority. Initially, I'll look for a positive message. But, even a bad message has a silver lining — so essentially, it is still positive.

What the heck was I so angry about? In retrospect, my anger was pure selfishness, with a side of mommy is a punk. I knew our relationship. I knew that she would continue to call and text me thirty times a day. I knew that Tai would always consult with me if she ever needed or wanted anything. So, I wasn't concerned there. All I had to do was be available. I did just that. I had to let her do this — be it a mistake or not! I had to be supportive and show her my support and encourage the best for both of them — her and her girlfriend. It was the same girlfriend that she had for a couple of years. During the pep talks from my mom and husband, they said, "It's actually a good thing that she wants to be independent. Don't make her feel bad about it!" I was like duh, hold on! It really is a good thing. She was responding to the direction that she'd been given by her parents. I was stuck being a selfish mother and I was ego-tripping. Everyone can use a pep talk every now and then. I needed mine.

I apologized to Tai and told her that my poor response was from the fear of shifting the household energy — it was all due to the fear of her energy dissolving all together and her not being part of our quad. Tai received my concerns with empathy and understanding. We were back in the sack like sisters and she was happily engaging again. Now, she was planning house shopping. I'm really a softy and Tai finally knew how to exploit me as she grew up. She knew that cooking anything was a good gesture to get whatever she wanted. She prepared several meals with hopes to ensue contributing to her home — that's for sure! Tai's incentive worked because, within a couple of days, I was online at IKEA ordering goods for her. I was trying to help prep as much as I could to get her comfortable. My disposition, regarding Tai's move, made a complete turnaround.

Arrangements were made to break my lease. As a result, Prince and I were preparing to leave the first week of April 2015. Though the current apartment that Tai and I had would be available, her girlfriend had paid the first month of rent in advance. Therefore, Tai would be moving into her new place within a couple of days and staying with me until I departed. Her new complex was about ten minutes away which was great because my mother was still in Florida.

I remember the last days so vividly. I can almost smell that day — the day that we left each other. I can smell the cleaning product scents, the candles, and the hot porterhouse rolls that I left behind in the oven. We departed with Tai around 5 in the morning because I had to go to Miami for business, but we were texting the entire time at sixty words per minute. Tai went over to my mother's house in the interim and hung out as she waited for her girlfriend to complete her drive down.

By noon the next day, it would be Tai's time to play house, except with the right intentions. It was with the intentions of becoming an independent woman on her own — in her own space with her own responsibilities. I was comfortable with everything. Plus, I knew that my mother was always within close reach.

The initial adjustment went smooth though I barely heard about it. Ironically, Tai didn't have as much time for me as I thought she would. At least, at first, she didn't. It was understandable though. She was so overwhelmed by work and the move. She was distracted, working, still getting settled and trying to maintain a household. I was not a priority. I guess being an adult was time-consuming for her. I would annoy her by sending repetitive long-winded messages like, "Helllllllllloooooooooooooooo, Taiiiiiiiiiiiiiiiiiiii!" so I could get her attention. Tai would respond, "Pleeeeaassssseee stop!" She wouldn't acknowledge my initial wants. She would just mimic me. Tai was very preoccupied during those days unless she needed me. When mommy rescue was in need, I'd better stop what I was doing and tend to her. That was our dynamic. I mean, in all honesty, my girlfriends' relationships would have suffered if Tai were physically here. We literally and willingly dominated each other's time. Tai and I came before anyone or anything sometimes. My kid was never too old to hang with me.

The ride home from Florida was surreal without her presence in the car; it was just too odd to take in at that moment. I felt weird. I felt as if I was leaving her behind. I kind of felt like I was turning my back on her — something that plays on my psyche all the time! But it was something that I was forced to do. I had to be comfortable with leaving without her. I was content for a bit because I knew that she would be visiting New York for Easter — that would be in two weeks. So, I was breathing a little easier. When I was able to get over foolishly sulking from Tai actually growing up, I was able to remember my endeavors (the seeds that I planted already). I had written a relationship book the year prior that needed editing, my husband and I were in the final stages of opening a new juice bar, and came to realize that I was ready to develop our brand.

We finally reached home and I was beyond glad! I was grateful to God that the ride was over. I was so happy to be home where I did not have to hear any more down South music! I'm a New Yorker through and through. I can't listen to that style continuously for hours. I will go crazy!

My husband and I pulled into the garage and began unloading. Shortly after, anxiously, I ran to be greeted by the arms and warm body of my loving son who I hadn't spent much time with or seen since last Christmas. I'd only really seen him through our FaceTime communications.. He was definitely missing his mommy, although I'm sure he'd beg to differ. He looked very thin like he had missed a few meals. His rib cage was actually showing. Noah was genuinely missing my nurturing. He was a sophomore in high school after all. Of course, he needed me! Noah needed the same treatment that I gave to his sister when she was in high school. Therefore, being able to provide the same for him was a definite incentive for moving back. The day my husband and I drove twenty hours back from Florida, we signed a lease and literally moved into a brand new development.

At that time, we lived in a new and crisp two bedroom, three bathroom townhouse. We bought new furniture again because this new place was too small to provide space for our old furniture that was already in storage from the Ritz. I was back in Westchester, living the suburban lifestyle. I was glad because, thankfully, it was a continuation of the Floridian warm weather.

It was spring in New York and I was able to workout outdoors which allows my soul to thrive. The solar energy gives me superhuman strength and I'm able to receive data from genuinely connecting with the universe. It is my absolute favorite pastime. I took these moments very seriously. I walked from White Plains to Yonkers once. And, in my town, that's sixteen miles! I loved every branch, leaf, and pebble that I passed along my trail; it was truly euphoric for me. Nature is the best therapy ever. After the three or four miles my endorphins were flowing allowing inadvertent messages to pour in.

Sometimes, the universe suggests one specific message or several messages. I'm always open, willing, and excited to receive mine. My mind opened up and the universe spoke to me on this day, transmitting a really strong premonition! The message was that I'm going to die within the next week. I'm not sure how or from what, but I had a strong feeling of dying and leaving my family behind. I abruptly stopped and reviewed a few things in my mind. Then, I immediately turned to my husband and said, "Baby, don't get scared, but something may happen to me next week." He was really confused. He replied, "huh?"

He was wearing his typical look of confusion, forehead creased with lines and brows bunched. I said, "No seriously, honey! This just came to me." Then, we had one of our extensive spiritual talks. I received the memo and I let it go. I certainly wasn't about to spend the rest of my day harping on my short future. It was such a beautiful and clear sunny day — where the sun was reflecting off the water and the lush spring greenery was kicking in. I continued my exercise and had an excellent workout that day.

CHAPTER 11

Love Never Dies

Noah, my husband and I were finally fully settled in our new home and enjoying the heat of Summer in New York. It was an especially exciting time because the 2015 BET Awards were coming up and The LOX were performing. Therefore, my husband would be on stage alongside Puff, Lil' Kim and the rest of the Bad Boy family. What a throwback it would be! I'm not sure what was more fascinating, the irony of them performing together again after all this time or the déjà vu. Either way, I was looking forward to the show.

I began looking for a dress for the red-carpet weeks ago. I decided on an Alice + Olivia piece. It was a stunning off-white brocade pattern baby doll dress. I had my packages sent weeks in advance from, my angel on earth, Dannie. This is not my roomie from Harlem. This Dannie who worked for Alice + Olivia. Through all my preparations, I was not off the parental mommy hook just yet. Amidst all the frenzy, I still kept in constant contact with Tai.

By now, she was about settled and had reintroduced me back into her life. I would consult with her regarding all of my fits, hair, and makeup. Makeup was Tai's forte; she learned new things daily from the tutorials she'd watch on YouTube. I always consulted with her and she would be there to oblige. Ahh, the perks of having a daughter! Tai was quick to tell me, "Ma, stop buying the same things! You have the same colors in your closet." The thing is, Tai was right — she was very observant and precautionary. She was my extra set of eyes. Securely, I knew that I was always good to go with her approval! Tai confirmed my ensemble, the details, and made sure that my look was made to perfection. Next, it was time to focus on my husband's look. He didn't need help with styles per se, he just needed help with organization and timing. He's constantly working. So, he doesn't know whether he's coming or going. Literally!

That's where I come in because clothing threads of any kind are my forte. Since my husband was performing, his stage outfit was covered through the stylist already. Therefore, my job was to provide an outfit for traveling prior to the performance and for the possible after party. Mr. Styles was actually in California for rehearsal and due back in New York the next evening. He was on the last leg of LOX's Trinity Tour as well. I was at home preparing for his return, cooking per usual, doing laundry, and running errands. I used the last few days to prepare for the performance.

Thursday, June 25, 2015. I woke up pretty early, before 8:00 am, missing the usual warmth that came from my husband's side of the bed. When he's away I struggle to keep my eyes closed for the night and certainly into the morning too. I'm surprised I'd slept at all; suffering from my own brand of separation anxiety. My morning routine consisted of calling hubby immediately upon waking up and before moving out of bed. From there, I made my daily organic smoothie consisting of kale, chard, frozen strawberries, vegetable protein powder, a squeeze of lemon, chia seeds, and diluted apple juice. Then, I prepared to walk Madonna, my beautiful black Patterdale Terrier that my husband bought some time ago while I was away in Florida. I must admit that I was a bit jealous of her, at first, because of their connection and her ignorance toward me. I knew that we would get close once she got a real dose of my energy.

She has provided a comfort that humans just cannot supply. The healing and love that Madonna offers was so unusual yet so satisfying. What isn't satisfying is her waiting at the foot of my bed, staring like a maniac to go for a walk — as she did this very moment. The walk would be a mixture of things — some exercise for me, some exercise for her, and detective work; one of my favorite things to do while I get fresh air. I'll be honest and say that a rapper's girlfriend makes the best detective; I've been trained.

Nonetheless, I made my way outside. I was familiar with the area, just not the street I lived on. Madonna and I were going to go went on a journey down this new street together in search of anything, honestly. I was still getting familiar with faces, dogs, and homes in this new move for our family.

I made a right out of our complex and adjacent to us stood another complex. It was an older styled area with residents who seemed to have lived there for decades. Their eyes were glued to the new Styles in the neighborhood and when walking Madonna, the stares of seniority were peppered within every block. I began to walk on the communal lawn and the glances transformed into bulging eyes, which grew more intense the further I walked down the street. While minding my business, I proceeded to keep walking my dog, sh*t bag in tow and tried not to make any more eye contact. I didn't want there to be any altercations. It was too early and Westchester cops and black people just don't mix. As I slowly began to move and walk in one direction, a tall slender man charged after me yelling and screaming. He yelled at the top of his lungs, telling me to get off the lawn.

I couldn't quite make out what he said but he proceeded to scream something about *black*. I told him to politely shut up and not to approach me as he had. I don't know what the something black meant or what he was referring to. Honestly, he could have been talking about the dog, but I had no clue and I didn't like his tone or body language. I walked off and called the police. I wanted documentation of racial slurs, before any further drama transpired. The police came over, prepared a report, and it was done. However, I didn't appreciate the negative energy so early in the morning.

As soon as I entered my home, I received a text from my daughter, Tai. It was around 10:20 AM.

"I'm tired of my girlfriend's shit. We're breaking up and I want to come home."

She was contacting me from her girlfriend's phone. The next message came through, "I'm leaving the house. Don't respond on here, but I will call you."

I received similar text messages before, so I wasn't too alarmed. I was more confused at the "don't respond," because now I had to wait. But, I did.

As the mother of a young adult, I have learned the hard way to respect my daughter's wishes. Plus, my mom was still in Florida where Tai now lived. My mother is retired and seemingly always available. I wouldn't wait too long but I wanted to give Tai some time and was afraid of treating her like an infant too soon. However, the text messages didn't sit well with me, especially after my negative exchange with the slender man just minutes ago. My antennae were up as Madonna paced her way around the kitchen floor. It's too early for people to be so miserable. I left the text alone for the moment believing Tai just needed a little time. I escaped to the hair salon - a place of refuge for many women I knew. My husband and I were leaving the next day for Los Angeles. Therefore, a hair and a lunch date with a friend in the city were on the books. However, throughout the next few hours, my antennae never retreated.

After some time had passed, I reached out to Tai and received no response. Having a young adult daughter means balancing their independence with your motherly instincts. I then reached out to her girlfriend's phone and still received no answer. I wasn't too worried just yet. I wrapped up what I was doing downtown and proceeded to head home.

Once finally inside, I tried to calm my mind and immediately began to peel the potatoes for my infamous vegan potato salad. I cut up the potatoes, threw them in the boiling pot and went upstairs to wrap up my hair to avoid the steam, food scents and the grease from latching on. I changed from my outside clothes to pajama pants and a tee, then went back down to the kitchen to really get my hands dirty. Hubby was en route home so I wanted to ensure that a hot meal awaited him. It was Thursday, a school day. Therefore, I knew that my son Noah would come through the door at any moment — only to drop his things off, kiss me, and double back out the door. I was messing around in the kitchen, trying to figure out what else I'd cook when it dawned on me that I hadn't heard back from Tai. I started to worry slightly and proceeded to text her multiple times. "Where is she?!" I said aloud to no one. Tai is the type of person who won't hesitate to call and ask for assistance if she needs help or is in trouble. So, I didn't take my worry to the deep end, treading lightly among frustration.

"Hi, Ma!" It was Noah, surely bursting through the door. He's my little saint, smiling with his perfect teeth, greeting me happily, as always. It was a two-second privilege that he gave before bolting straight to his room. Computers, video games, dirt bikes, and girls ran his world. Only Noah knew what was on his extracurricular to-do list. Unfortunately, I had to interrupt his after-school planning so that I could harass him to walk Madonna as I continued cooking.

One hour later, with a meal almost complete, a few knocks on the door pulled me from the kitchen. I walked to the front of the house wondering, who could this be? I looked through the peephole and a police uniform looked back at me. There were two men — one outfitted as an officer and the other in a plain white shirt. I couldn't make out if the man in the white shirt was a cop or not.

"Who is it?" I said as if I couldn't see who stood beyond the door. I needed verbal confirmation. They replied, almost in unison, "White Plains Police Department." Luckily, I hadn't just hit a joint. Finally, ready to comply, I reached to open the door. Just before I turned the lock, I thought to abruptly ask, "May I help you?" I'm no criminal and I didn't have any cases. Therefore, I didn't do anything — not to mention that my husband wasn't home.

One of the officers said, "We need to come in and speak to Mrs. Styles." I peculiarly replied, "How do you know my name?"

The officers and I went back and forth a bit because I wanted clarification for their visit prior to opening the door. I was intrigued. Though I gave in and finally allowed them to come in

"Does this have anything to do with my neighbors from earlier?" I immediately asked. They said no. I apologized for being a bit hasty and during my apology, I realized that the other man who was wearing the white shirt was in fact a cop — he looked like the head of the department. They gave me the impression that cops only disturb the neighborhood for serious incidents.

He turned to me and asked, "Are you Tai Hing's mother?"

"Yes." I replied.

He then said his name which is a complete blur and proceeded to tell me, "Your daughter was pronounced dead at 11:30 this morning."

I can't even begin to explain what I was feeling. My only response was, "Whaaaaaat? Noaahh! Noaaaaah! Come, come. Wait, what officer? How is this possible? She just texted me this morning! This is a mistake. How would you know?! She isn't even in NY?" He said, "I know. She was in Florida and that's where she passed."

I somewhat believed him then — not coherently though!

"Nooooooooooooooooo, not my baby!" I started screaming and crying, dropped to the floor, and I began to grab the ankles of both officers. They were trying their best to console me. But, at that moment, there was no consoling. I was done and, in another dimension — weirded the fuck out to be honest.

I yelled, "Do you have kids? What am I supposed to do now officers? Tell me! Tell me!"

Noah grabbed my shoulder, soft but stern. He walked me over to the couch and sat me down while I was in horrific shock! My stomach, brain, and heart had all been trampled on and I was in so much immediate physical pain. Noah was so casual, calm, and cool. He just placed me down. There was no way that he wasn't jolted by that whammy too. In retrospect, I know that he was really protecting me by all measures. The father, husband, and son mannerisms kicked in and really took over in that situation. I was too confused and totally disconnected from myself instantly. I couldn't keep still. I couldn't stop crying. I couldn't stop trying to make calls; all the while just wanting Tai first and my husband second.

Noah was now communicating with the officers on his own accord. I remember hearing one say, "Is she going to be okay?! Is it safe to leave?!"

Noah responded, "Yes, absolutely! I will take care of her!!" Awww, my baby! As sick as I was, his maturity and protection registered right away. Noah gave me a piece of my heart back immediately with that move; my little man. My kids have always reciprocated love, but Noah really surprised me and amazed me beyond words! His support for me made my lack of support for him more evident. I wanted to be there for him. I needed to be there for him. Ironically, God flipped the tables. And, I'm so thankful and admire Noah's strength to this day. Quite honestly, I've admired his strength ever since. Noah has demonstrated and maintained a strength that most adults don't even possess. And, I thank God every single day for him and for having met his father.

Now, I'm playing the waiting game. I was waiting for Hubby to arrive. He was returning on a flight from LAX to LGA. That's basically 6-7 hours of travel time in total. With every second came more pain. It was as if the knife that was stuck in my heart was being turned and plunged in deeper and deeper. I contacted my mother immediately, mainly because she was in Florida and I wanted to know what the f*ck was going on down there. I startlingly explained what happened. Her first response was shock. Then, she inquisitively said, "I missed a call from Tai earlier this morning...interesting." My mother's response was at best very odd. However, I didn't even connect the two yet. So, I gave her the details and she began to make calls.

I called my girlfriends and they immediately rushed over — balling and hyperventilating, they came over to the house one by one. Tiffany left work, rushed over in scrubs and was in hives already due to the news. I almost had to literally call an ambulance for her. In the interim, I was still ignorantly trying to somehow get through to my husband, knowing that he's in the air and unavailable. Yet, I kept trying and leaving messages. Jamal came by with a distraught, wrinkled, and red face of sheer confusion, crying. It was like he hadn't heard me the first time. So, he asked, "What did you say?!" My other girlfriend, Sofi, came by, not knowing anyone, because she's from D.C., trying to find a way to support, she started cleaning and tended to my dog, Madonna. She kept uttering, "I'm...I'm just not good with death." I needed no explanation. Her presence was enough! The love was evident immediately. My other girlfriend, Quia, came over, really trying to keep it together and then she lost it. She said, "I just can't believe this." A few others came by and by the time that I looked around, they needed more help than I did and now I was the one consoling everyone else. I did feel their pain too. It was horrible. A horrible feeling. A horrible day. And, we were all looking at each other like what do we do now?

I've never felt so vulnerable and juvenile in my adult life. I felt like a child. I felt like someone who had lost their blanky or favorite toy. I felt like a lost kid, resonating to the time when I went to live with my dad and left my mom with my abusive stepdad. It felt as though my life was out of my control, knowing that she was going to get mistreated the moment that we left. I felt the stress of her stress. Tai's passing was a black and white change for me that was too drastic. I immediately felt stifled and was suffocating from life itself. It was arduous to breathe. It was as if air consisted of my reality and my body would automatically reject any attempts to inhale. I just didn't want to accept this new truth. I wanted immediate peace at that moment and for the future. I wanted to be wrapped up in a heated blanket of security and love. I didn't want to be in my reality.

My whole family dynamic had changed in a snap. My whole world flipped upside down. Perhaps, Tai's stress was because of her insatiable need for independence. The move was like going from 0-100 for her, meaning that she was now being the provider and was basically over it the moment that her adult life began. Maybe it was a complete shock. Tai had no practical idea of what it meant to live alone — let alone with anyone else. I tried to reiterate this to her. But I had to let her explore. I believe that she would have been more successful if she had an immediate support system in place. She wasn't emotionally stable, and she was just too far from home.

Hubby flew in the door and stood in the doorway waiting. I swiftly ran up to greet him. His arms were open wide, and his eyes were practically swollen shut from crying. We immediately hugged hard and tight. He was crying and chanting, "What happened? What happened?" I was saying, "What are we going to do? Baby Tai is gone!" It went back and forth!

We just stood there with bleeding hearts, rocking back and forth, and hugging one another. It was a parent's worst nightmare. Apparently, he received the messages that I left upon landing, which was so stupid. I could have given him a heart attack. As we were holding each other, he noticed that I had company over. However, at this time, they had to leave. My husband is very private and proud. He really needed and wanted to be alone with his immediate family. So, he thanked everyone for coming to my aid and excused everyone. I was basically just floating around (definitely off weed), but it felt literal to me. It was like I started to view myself, looking at my life, instead of being in it. I was hovering over it all like a ghost. Right away, I started feeling a sense of relief for Tai. But the pain wouldn't allow me to stay focused on the relief. I went in and out with emotion, not really gauging or grasping my emotions because they were too erratic. However, the hoovering feeling remained.

I took a breath in the middle of a tear like, "whew!" It was the breath that you take after a long run, workout, or after a long workday. It was as if it was finally over. Of course, it wasn't the feeling of Tai's life being over. No, but it was the feeling of contentment. She was at home and at peace. She was no longer worrying about anything or missing anyone. There was no more pain or disappointment! There was no more having to live up to anyone's standards. She was officially free!

Now, I feel, as a mother, I can admire her because she's more powerful now than ever before. She feels even more necessary and important! She feels as though she is in a place where she can see her growth, input, and knowledge in others. As she evolves, we evolve; it shows that we, as a family on earth, benefit!

We decided to fly out to Florida the next day. I was sadly sickened, distraught, and dreading it. But I had to go and clean out Tai's apartment, sign papers, and handle looming responsibilities there. I was gearing up my emotions for that deal. I didn't contact Mike. One, because I didn't have his contact. Two, because a social media message wasn't the right delivery. And, three, they weren't on my radar because, again, no one was in contact with anyone. But I knew that they knew. How could they not? I got the confirmation when Mike's wife sent me a text on the next day. He obviously knew. The world knew by the next day due to my husband being a celebrity. His sister, the aunt, eventually reached out in shock, as expected, but all I wanted was to come together in love. That was the time that you show up and try to really implement yourself and repent. We honestly hoped that he or someone would have met us out in Florida as well. We needed support too! I honestly grew angry at this point. And, I really didn't want to deal with any of them, realizing that I am a priority now — my health, physically and mentally. So, anything that was challenging was not a priority! In addition, I felt that it was now a privilege to know anything new about Tai. Conveniently, they've had access to her, but they didn't take advantage of it when she was alive. I wanted to protect my baby and I felt like I could finally.

Upon arriving in Florida, I met up with my mother. She had already started some preliminary work down there. She had been conversing with the officers, the morgue, and was acting as a stand-in making decisions until we had arrived. I was dreading the whole flight experience and flat out wondering how the hell I was going to get through! By this time, most of the public had heard the news. Walking through the airport with my husband was literally torture. I could not stop crying and because all eyes were on us. I thought, *can we just be human — without the stares and autographs?* I get that people were sad as well, but, imagine us! Your sadness may fade, but this was our new life. We needed a moment to settle into it.

My husband and I landed on Friday mid-morning. Noah stayed back for obvious reasons. What I knew for sure was that

Tai had a bad day and that I was going to figure out why and how. I was going to make some sense out of it. The Florida air had a weird aura to it. It felt bizarre. It was as if there was a scent of her in the air. Maybe it was the familiarity of scents from the places that we frequented together — either way, it didn't make me happy! It was way too eerie and weird. I could feel her, but just not see her. And, it seemed like she was trying to tell me something somewhere. It was surreal and very hard to explain I felt as though I was in a constant state of wonder, thinking that the answer will fall out of the sky at any time.

Honestly, my first thoughts were, *what the hell went on in that damn house?* First things first, "Was Tai murdered and was it covered up?" This was my thought because we were literally in a town where you could get away with murder. It's a slower-paced, antiquated modern town; basically, old ways with new designs. I knew that Tai's girlfriend was way too sweet and cool for that (murder that is). Her love with Tai was so devoted. Therefore, I couldn't process the thought. My motherly instincts wouldn't allow me to believe that anyway. But I couldn't help but think of all of this.

When something tragic happens, your mind goes all over the place. We went over to the apartment, cleaned it out, and packed up all the important pieces. And, from the looks of the apartment, the only murder was in the fridge, a carcass — big dead pot roast. I continued looking around. The house was kept. The dishes were loaded the night before and the laundry was done. She was big on keeping the house; so, the apartment was clean, and everything was situated and mirrored how she was raised. It was sad, but cute to see because this was her first apartment. Everyone remembers their first apartment! This was hers. She had taken our old furniture, which really wasn't old at all and moved it into her new place. I painted a picture for her prior to leaving Florida and it was hanging on the wall. There was a balcony with a view. The apartment was cute. My investigating took a turn when I started to look in the cabinets and more into the fridge.

I thought, "Ooommmggg! I knew it!" I knew that something was off with this situation! There was nothing but high sodium, sugary, sweet dye in the house aka Walmart groceries! Aka drugs! Yes, bad food is a drug! There it was, clear as day, blue drink was in the fridge along with franks, canned cabbage, and some gross looking roast. Yuck! That's just promoting erratic, hyper-ness, and impulsiveness — which I know for a fact, contributed to her thoughts that morning or weeks prior to for that matter. Tai came from an organic vegan household. No, she wasn't a vegan. But, she damn near was — drinking water was a hobby and so was cramming ourselves with vitamins and nutrients. So, this diet was a complete shock to her system along with the weed and liquor because our diets are the key to creating neurotransmitters.

Neurotransmitters are the brain chemicals that communicate information throughout your brain and body. These transmitters tell your heart to beat and your stomach to digest. My point is that Tai wasn't eating nutrient rich foods, as she used to, that would have allowed her to feed her brain and body the balance that was needed. They would have stabilized her mood. A healthy diet would have never been the culprit. Eating high processed foods, not only depletes your energy, but over time, if you're dependent on it, it interferes with the normal brain chemistry. My kid needed some pineapples and nuts (serotonin boosters), with a side of working out, to get those endorphins released! This would have made positive impacts on her lifestyle. It was a combination of emancipation, munchies and alcohol that brought Tai to her demise. I don't judge. I smoke weed and drink on occasion. But, it's always about balance. If you're going to drink and smoke, then at least rehydrate and replenish what you're removing when drinking and smoking or it's going to warp your body — sooner or later!

Overanalyzing, I started to make sense of some things. The girlfriend stated that they had an argument and Tai thought that they were breaking up. All those emotions combined with the diet, plus being away from home with the feelings of being single and possibly neglected, came to play. I am sure Tai grew depressed. She was away from everyone. Tai felt helpless with no recourse. And, what saddens me the most was her strength. In retrospect, she put on a front for me and for everybody. She wouldn't tell me how much or how bad she was hurting. She wouldn't complain at all. Knowing her, Tai wanted to be mature. Pride has been my downfall too, but I had to get over that when the hospital almost retained me. Nevertheless, Tai only complained of a few spats in her relationship. I sincerely wasn't concerned. There was no need to be.

The actual report stated suicide in the apartment. But I'm still hoping it's something else, oddly. I didn't know. Perhaps, they somehow got the details messed up. I wasn't sure where it took place in the apartment. So, I called Tai's girlfriend for clarification. No, she didn't shoot herself, cut herself, or take pills. She hung herself, which actually says a lot about Tai's determination and will. I'm still in shock! It is still surreal. Tai's natural scent was now literally thick and sitting in the air — right in my nostrils! Then it hit me. This realization was buckling. We have both been stifled — "\choked in life. Tai was choked on her way out as I was choked on my way in. When I was born, my mother's umbilical cord wrapped around my neck so tightly that I almost died during birth. The doctor had to physically go in the womb and untangle the cord allowing oxygen to flow. I symbolically took that snafu as my physical not wanting to return to earth. As if I didn't want to be born and now my daughter had died by such a cord. I don't believe in coincidences, it's all synchronization.

My mother was having anxiety, trying to figure out if she can help or if she should have to wait in the car. My husband was trying to be the super strong man by moving around. Therefore, no one would witness the tears falling down his face — but I did, and it was agonizing. We were all a mess, but we were doing the best that we could.

My mother, husband, and I continued our painful paths. There were several priorities that needed handling: signing Tai's death certificate was one of them. Whatever was left of my heart completely dropped after I did that unbelievable act. Let me repeat. I had to sign my daughter's death certificate! Never in a zillion years could I have even dreamt of such wildness. The moment after it was signed, I was so hurt and even more broken. It was another extremely painful element to have to process. It was like putting a real nail in the coffin. Just when I thought that I was stable, a sharp but heavy borderline nauseous feeling of boiling anxiety and pain would take over. It made my head feel heavy; a pain in my chest accompanied by dizziness, probably from a lack of sleep. I felt a certain feeling leaving the precinct — a feeling that I didn't think was possible. However, I'm human. So, it did. I was on the highway, sitting in the backseat of the car. I tried opening the door, hoping that I could fall out on the highway and get run over. No shame here, I 100% did not want to be here, at all! I felt as such all the time back then, not just on this day either. I was over life and the future.

Fortunately, for me, my mother would have the child safety on for her adult grandkids. It wasn't my time to go meet Tai yet. However, I was so ready. After I couldn't get the door open, I just sat and thought. Horribly, every song that came on had to do with her somehow. The one that stood out the most was Fetty Wap. He was Tai's favorite artist. She knew about him before he became popular, even before her own dad, and he's in the music industry. Every third song that played was his and the ones in between all have meaning, I was able to be somewhat pleasantly distracted from my suicidal thoughts.

In the middle of a melodic head sway, I started to see the collateral beauty! I began to focus on the fact that my grandmother had just passed. So, why wouldn't they be together? My grandmother was ninety-two. She had a long and fruitful life. Of course, she'd show Tai the ropes. I knew that she was happier and in a better place. So, why wouldn't Tai be too? I did ponder quickly about the idea that she may go to hell because she took her own life. However, as soon as that came in, it went out. I don't beat myself up nor do I hold my standards to what another man says regarding Tai. I know how to receive my messages when I need them and it's not from a Bible. Although, there are some good stories and I have read it a bit. However, the Bible is not my go-to for enlightenment. One day, I'll get through the entire book, if I am called to do so.

As I got settled in my new position of *a mother who has lost a child*, I noticed that every single time I tried to pity myself or get deep in my feelings, it would be deflected. It still happens to this day. Having come back to Westchester, I'm now experiencing signs from Tai — signals that immediately derail me from crying. It's like she senses it and then remedies it because she doesn't want me suffering. Thankfully, I needed that because my mind was stuck going back and forth. I thought, "Well if she's gone and I take my life, then I'll be responsible for why she did what she did. Like mother, like daughter. I kept talking to myself after a deflection episode would happen to keep me on the lighter side of things. I would tell myself that the only thing for me to do now is to live for her and to live for me and to have her live through me!" I can't even say that I'll live for my husband and son, their importance will come in later. I can say, wholeheartedly, that they weren't a focus — because they weren't. I'm not saying that in a harmful way, but something was going on with me, something that perhaps they, the men, couldn't relate to.

It was evident to me that I was now in two places. I was in a spirit world and a human world. And, I could feel it. I didn't want to deal with my reality here just yet. I was trying to place Tai somewhere and then place myself where she was. *Where was she anyway? What stage is she in?* Because you don't just go straight to heaven (or toward the brightest light)! *Is she receiving my religious mirror messages that I leave her?* I was feeling at my lowest then. I was feeling so empty and hollow. I was already at the bottom. *What's worse than this?! Can anything be worse than this?*

Tai and I always talked about death, go figure. And, we would talk about death even more after my grandmother passed, which was ten months prior to her passing. My grandmother was cremated — one of the many wishes that she requested since forever. And, Tai hopped on that bandwagon. She adamantly said that she wanted to be cremated if anything should happen to her. It was a hint from God perhaps, but she said it. And, I made a mental note and said that I wanted the same for myself. I'm good on the funeral home beat face anyway. The gray/green ashy makeup? It's a no thanks for me and for Tai! I initially thought that my grandmother and I sparked the thought of cremation for her. As of now, I believe that Tai's decision may have been influenced by all the different cultures and religions that she studied. There are some correlations that I've noticed between Hinduism, suicide, and death. I remember that Tai was super enthused to learn, especially about Hinduism. Hence, the Ganesh tattoo that she had on her arm. Judaism intrigued her as well. She researched indigenous cultures and was obsessed with Anne Frank and the Holocaust for a while. From about twelve years old, she would bury herself in books, studying, and researching all on her own incentive.

During the first few weeks after Tai's passing, I couldn't feel much other than the pit that was lodged in my stomach and chest. I could only feel when I had overwhelming waves of uncontrollable sorrow that was buckling and so debilitating that I had to lie down. Besides those moments, I didn't feel much, not even the day that I went to buy Tai's cremation clothing. Of course, it's unbelievable, insane, and heinous, but I did it. I got her as cute as I could. My husband and mother went to the crematory and prepped Tai. I sent them first so that they can check out how she looked. Remember, Tai was shipped from Florida. Therefore, who knew what condition she would be in. I certainly didn't need any horrible images implanted in my mind. When my mother and husband returned, they insisted that I not go. They basically told me that they weren't allowing me. I never went to see Tai before she was cremated. I'm grateful that I didn't. I still have my jovial beautiful memories to refer to.

Tai was cremated and arrangements were made for the actual funeral service. The service was extremely sentimental even with the huge elephant in the room — Mike not being present. But, no one seemed to focus on that, which was good. I expected everyone to fall in line after my tragedy. However, this is my real life, my own journey and when I understood that notion, I understood to let go of all expectations. I've learned that I'm basically handicapped though you cannot see my impediment. The truth is that this is the worst pain and if you could identify with it, I doubt you'd spew any negativity. We have to let go of our expectations during our trials because it is via our determination and our own personal journey that we show up, day after day. Today, was mine.

The service was followed by a beautiful repass; it all seemed so final at that point. It was as if we were supposed to just close the door and it was over. Trying to begin to process this meant having to accept and process my mother's missed call from Tai.

During my own investigation, the facts revealed that Tai made those calls to her while under duress. Unfortunately, my mother missed the call. Tai reached out to her and I only. For a while, I would really ponder and try to put myself in Tai's shoes on the morning of the tragedy. I kept trying to trace her steps and, perhaps, think of what she was possibly thinking. Either way, I knew that there was no end to the pain in sight — at all. I was fully drenched in it.

Unfortunately, for me and for us, this was when the real nightmare set in.

PART III

CHAPTER 12

Seeking Spirit in a Long Island Medium

My sister randomly gave me a business card of a medium by the name of Lynn Leclere. She was given the card from her coworker, who also lost a child. I took this information as a blessing and a message. It was a no brainer for me to make the call. I wasn't raised with any particular religion. Therefore, I had no preconceived notions about the experience, only my own thoughts. I'd heard negatives and positives and conducted my own research. But, at this point, sitting on my bed every single day staring into oblivion, bursting into tears, not eating or sleeping, wasn't going to turn out well.

Every single day, everyone was asking or telling me I had to speak to someone. It was so damn annoying although I get that they were concerned. *But, why right away? What about if I didn't want to? Then, I'd be judged? Why are we always looking at doctors as if they were Gods?* They definitely know more because it's their arena and their area of expertise. However, one should verse themselves in a few things first before automatically assuming that you can't help yourself. Yes, this was an extraordinary case and maybe it seemed like it required some urgency to the next person, but this wasn't the case for me.

I wasn't ready to go sit in a room and talk to another human that had not experienced what I had just experienced. Gradually, in between the tears and pondering, I started doing research. I found chat groups of parents who not only lost their kids, but who had lost kids to suicide. I watched endless videos on clairvoyance and afterlife, which is why it was no surprise when God sent Lynn Leclere to me.

Honestly, I believe that a few spirits had hands in connecting Lynn to me. Tai knew that I needed her. It was the most expensive, yet priceless gift that I'm sure I will ever receive in this lifetime. I was feeling desperate. I knew that I wouldn't be any good to the world without some sense of closure and understanding because Tai and I were too close. I felt like I dropped the ball somehow. I kept saying, "How the f**k could this happen with me as the parent?" Or, I'd think about if there were any steps I'd missed.

I picked up the phone and made the call while thinking this is Tai bringing me to her...I know it is. To my surprise, the woman who was so pleasant, told me that she was booked for six months. I thought, I'm going to die by then! I was seriously stuck. Then, I told her that my daughter passed away and she said, "Oh no! This is urgent. You can come next week."

I was so happy and thankful; I knew that it was God and Tai! That alone made me feel a bit better inside. On the days leading up to my appointment, I was a little lighter in mood because I was in hopes of speaking to Tai and having a successful session. I prayed every night and all day when I remembered!

The day finally came to see Lynn.

She lived in Long Island which was about forty minutes away from us. It was essentially right there. From the moment that I approached her front door, I felt the light and the love of her energy. Sincerity and warmth immediately developed inside of me and I believe that it was her spirit speaking to me. I love how that happens, when a person communicates; speaks before they actually speak aloud. When I'm tuned in, I can gage the vibes, the energy, and the aura of a person.

Lynn was loving and kind. And, last but not least, she had an honest presence about her. I was blatantly anxious. I rambled and talked too much from the start. However, I felt completely comfortable and proceeded to take a seat. Lynn connected with Tai, my grandmother, my father-in-law, and my brother-in-law within seconds. She even connected with my husband's grandmother that he never met.

She began saying things that no one would know other than my husband and I. I recorded the entire session on tape. I was able to listen to my daughter tell me everything. Through Lynn's connection, Tai told me her fears, her concerns, and was abundantly apologetic for hurting herself and the family by doing what she did. She even had a message for her girlfriend. I felt as though I was having a literal conversation with Tai at times. The medium was an older woman, at least seventy years of age. However, she took on a juvenile disposition when connecting with Tai. It was totally bizarre, but I thoroughly embraced the session. It was such a gift that I was receiving. Some people will never get this experience, a true genuine reading. I've had generic psychic readings before, but this was my first medium experience and I felt beyond blessed.

"Tai is in a space of getting acclimated and returning to school," said Lynn as she sat looking into me with my daughter's spirit around her. This was an odd disclosure from the medium.

"Tai is also in a space of trying to forgive her father. Tai took her anger and animosity to the other side with her and they are working with her. She is trying to evolve, but the father's situation was stopping her. Tai needs to be in a space of forgiveness in order to move forward on another plane," I sat and listened as small goosebumps formed.

Additionally, Lynn told me that Tai had been particularly angered from what transpired, specifically during her memorial service. Nothing transpired other than her father not showing up. Sadly, he hadn't come, and Tai was privy to that. Mike's side of the family supported in large groups that day — just not Mike. This resulted in Tai being bothered, that was my analysis. Another analysis was that it said a lot about the significance of forgiveness.

Keeping in mind that Tai was a vivacious twenty-year-old young human, her information was pouring in. Lynn had more than a mouthful for me. So, happily, I recorded the two hour conversation. It was as if Tai couldn't wait to finally communicate with me. She even thanked me for my daily mirror messages consisting of her name within a heart. I thanked God continuously that day and every single day thereafter.

There were so many revelations — a lot of truths were being dumped on me. Tai said that she never knew how hard my life was as a child and how many situations I have conquered. Honestly, I neglected to mention them because I assumed that it was irrelevant. Plus, I have also tried not to focus on the cup being empty, but half full. So, I never dwelled.

Lynn continued, "Tai admires your strength." That acknowledgment made me chuckle because Tai believed I was raised how she was, which was in luxury and with many advantages. She just couldn't comprehend any other lifestyle.

It was in the fall when I visited her, specifically in October. Tai had waited four months for this. I was suffering greatly. Therefore, receiving those messages made it somewhat better. I have some advice if any of you want to plan a visit to go see a medium, don't go looking in the mirror if you can't handle your reflection. If you haven't lived your truth or accepted it, just don't

even look. That's what a good medium is; a sheer reflection. Whatever is in the dark will come to light at that time. I received an unexpected clarity about a select few truths. I had a faint relationship with God prior to Tai's transition. Therefore, I knew him, but I had no idea I'd get confirmation that there are other eyes in the sky. Tai, my grandmother, and brother-in-law are all guilty of spying on me and mine — and, I wouldn't have it any other way. I knew of my issues years ago and cleaned myself up, along with my husband doing work on himself too. There were no surprises for us at all.

Thankfully, God granted me three human mirrors. I'm constantly reflecting due to this. Lynn not only spoke of Tai's crossover, she also spoke to my relationship with Styles, and much more. A long-term relationship can only thrive from deep soul searching — something that requires willing participants. The good, the bad, and the ugly — my husband has regurgitated it back at me at some point in our relationship. Nonetheless, I was prepared to hear it and own it again. But I still kept an open mind because all of the information wasn't 100% accurate. However, mine was about 98% accurate.

Tai made me feel safe with the words, "There was nothing that I could have done. I'm the best mother ever." Tai dispatched those messages to me, and I needed to hear them. I mean, I knew who I was at one point in my life. But, when your child commits suicide, you begin to question your whole existence. Tai even went on to say how she was at peace and was okay, specifically, when asked.

"I am with G2," she added and that was the final straw and the ultimate feeling of security. Hallelujah! At this point, I was feeling so blessed and thankful that I got what I needed for now. Lynn, the medium, isn't there to tell you what you want to hear either. She gives it to you straight — like when she told me that I smoked too much weed. That was all facts. She then said that it was probably a result of the anxiety that I had. I didn't know that I was suffering from anxiety and after the tip, I researched and understood the severity of my case.

Lastly, she threw in how I am impatient with my husband sometimes and that I needed to be easier on him. Now, she was revealing too much. This isn't about him! But I listened with a facetious ear and one eyebrow up. Although my husband didn't require the experience, he liked

hearing that.

We left gloating. Hubby said, "I already told you most of that." At the same time he spoke he rolled his eyes. He did tell me most of what I received. I just couldn't listen to him and take his word for it. I needed more information and for it to be certified, in a sense. That was something that the medium provided.

I went to speak to someone after all. It was my kind of someone.

CHAPTER 13

The Privilege of Losing My Child

The privilege of losing my child sounds like an oxymoron to most. Personally, that's the only way to really categorize my situation — as a privilege. Being a parent is one obvious privilege because you're the chosen one. You've been given a special right to be a parent. You have been granted a job and a chance to raise humans. It is a luxury that can be taken away at any point or not even granted at all. Therefore, since I was chosen to haul such a profound emotional baggage through life, I've been given another right — the privilege of being used as a muse. A kind of physical strength for others to observe because what sincerely hasn't killed me, made me stronger — an awareness and new consciousness, through belief and prayer, is attainable.

God is the provider and the taker of life. I believe this wholeheartedly. Have you ever considered the thought of losing your child? Most likely not. And, if you're feeling like your stomach has dropped out, then you're probably considering it now. It's easy to have and raise kids into the physical but try maintaining a mandated spiritual relationship with your child when they are gone! That is a totally different experience. I am still Tai's mother. She is still watching me, therefore I'm not off the hook. I still have to be an honorable upstanding parental figure and I believe by doing so she elevates. Only God can bless you with the major task and lifestyle that parenting in the physical provides. And, only God knows the strength that you must possess in order to move forward, to eventually be a muse if they're gone. It becomes a kind of rebirth with a gift of newfound strength and endurance that most will never comprehend or be granted the privilege to bear. That's the privilege!

I had no idea of the advantages of being a parent when my kids were young. This advantage was simply the fact of having little remnants of your DNA running around, in a new or old soul, while being packaged in a human shell. I thought that they were sent to me so that I could be the guiding force through this life — a kind of an authoritative figure. Though, a small percentage of that rings true, it is quite the contrary. They are actually here to teach us, keep us mindful of a lot, and to keep us grounded. It works both ways. I began to see the privilege when things came full circle after Tai transitioned. She made herself present most often — in trying times, happy times, or even just the simplest of times. I believe that I needed to keep reinforcing the lessons that she bestowed when she was here in the physical. For example, if I should get distracted by being human and fall into negativity or intend to be annoyed by another's frivolous actions, I believe that a sign or synchronicity would appear. This frequently alluded to e subliminal messages for me not to sweat the small stuff! She is my angel and does her work as such! I've received so many jewels and treasures after Tai's passing. One that rings loud, "Live to the fullest! Everything is temporary…people, places, emotions, and things. All temporary!" I have acknowledged my awareness and the need to be different (to live in the present) by diligently working and striving to be the best human that I can be.

Oddly, Tai's transition was the demolition that I needed. I needed a demolition of myself in order to see the diamond that I was. Tai's death has given me new life. I needed to be completely stripped of everything that was easy and comforting in order to be broken down to the core. After the reading with Lynn, I dived deeper into a spiritual and mental paradigm shift. I needed to build myself up again. It was like Lego art — a beautifully constructed, yet delicate, piece that, most times, gets erroneously demolished for some unforeseen reason.

That was me. To see that Tai was on a barter — I'm eternally grateful. Lynn also told me about past lives — Tai's past life to be exact. This caused me to explore more into the subject matter. Everything in life is basically a choice. You are given options to believe in whatever resonates within you. And, the deeper that I got into my beliefs of spirituality, the more I saw the connections and synchronicities that worked for me. I've learned that we are all here on a loan. Just because your child comes through you, it does not mean that the child is yours. I am just a vessel hosting a spirit — an entity that has had many other lives with other parents. Learning that your husband could have been your son or father in another life is both amazing and gross at the same time, to be honest. Yet, I'm here for it. I am here to accept all the grossness and weirdness to get to where I'm going (a place of peace). I was thankful for the validation of knowing that everything I've done and everything that is happening is deliberate! It is all a part of the plan. There are no coincidences and no mistakes. Situations, trips, and occurrences were all done to reinforce the family and promote quality time! Nothing was done in vain. I was truly thankful for my awareness at such an early age.

I sincerely believe that my privilege was only attained through resilience and perseverance, a burning desire to not let life quietly happen to me. I didn't fold, I didn't give up, and I believed in something positively greater than myself. Of course, it wasn't easy. Of course, I was totally unaware, and I didn't know my elbow from my assh*ole anymore. Living after your child passes is like living with a bullet inside of you. You never forget and begin to just live with the pain. Yet, this obstacle, like all, has led me to something greater. I strapped up, by arming myself spiritually, emotionally, and mentally; soul searched, and paid attention to all of my messages from the universe. Hence, I was living life in the present.

I had no impractical expectations, because I'm still working on it, all the while understanding that this life is temporary. Having had to delve into the core of my utter existence by being broken to become whole again is just simply transformational. Through that, I've been given a gift of enlightenment.

Everyone is allotted the opportunity to use trauma or another hardship to get to their place of peace, purpose, or their happy place. The option, the gift to self-reward, is granted to everyone. I'm no one special, no hero — we are all God's children and we possess abilities that we have no knowledge of, most times until we are faced with adversity. It's what one does with that adversity that exposes who you really and truly are. If you are going through any kind of stress, please stay in the light. You are going through it for a reason! Allow your flower (your temple and spirit) to fully blossom.

At first, it hurts beyond recognition — beyond being able to see forward or in any direction. Then, it changed me, and will change you forever! My bittersweet privilege.

CHAPTER 14

Honoring the Mind, Body, and Soul

Taking priority and care of your mental state should be preached from the time that you're able to comprehend what a brain is and the weight of all of its functions. Unfortunately, it's not. Inadvertently, most people have learned about their mental status through a doctor, a teacher, or by judgement and ridicule. Gratefully, experts have finally convinced people to believe and understand that mental health is a priority and there's no good physical health without a solid balance of mental health.

Instantly a barrage of "was she crazy?" questions followed the moment after I mentioned that I lost my daughter to suicide. They said, *"What was wrong with her? Was she depressed?"* They always ask so many things. Obviously, something was wrong with her that day and clearly she was depressed! How the heck would I ever know? Was that her life? No!

Would the feeling have subsided later? Absolutely. But, having acted off impulse and feelings of being alone with no real support, it ultimately was the catalyst for her demise. Also, taking into consideration how we, as a community, have been taught to view mental health and illness as taboo, it doesn't make for a comfortable table discussion! We aren't God, yet we judge other people's decisions every single day. Then, we, humans, go to church and worship what another person is preaching to make ourselves feel better about those same judgments. Oy vey! It's a never-ending cycle of not honoring yourself.

Even doctors who are educated, were trained by someone else who was trained by someone else, and it continues. Their word still isn't the gospel! At what point do we introduce God, genetics, and common sense? The Creator has provoked those thoughts — whether you want to agree with it or not. It's not your doing. It's the divine who plays a crucial role — just like my husband always reinforces with the yin and yang philosophy. It states that everything has darkness and lightness to it. I believe in that way of thinking because for me, it seems so logical. Considering you have no actual handicap issues, God will always give you choices. It's up to us to take advantage of them. I trust that Tai was given choices as well — either she was in the dark and couldn't see the light, so. He relieved her or after one of God's angels finished their task at hand (being physical love), she returned home. Unambiguously, who can beg to differ?

There are two perspectives that I consider when it comes to Tai; fate or a model of physical love concealed by emotional angst. Fate was due to God being the ultimate giver and taker of life. The emotional angst and love may be because God used Tai for a sacrificial purpose — knowing that on the exterior she seemed happy yet on the interior she was suffering and making everyone that interacted with her examine their influence or lack thereof. This allowed her to leave her messages and stamp them with love and then return home. Maybe she was here for a purpose? The purpose of love. That is how I chronicle her and her transition. People attempt suicide every single day and there are accidents every single day. However, they all aren't fatal, which is why I stated earlier that you may view Tai's decision a little differently. With an open mind. In terms of that being her journey, it was already written for her. God has the answers.

Mental health means exactly what it says. It is the health of the mind, which is our emotional, psychological, and social well-being. It affects how we think, feel, and act. It also helps determine how we handle stress, relate to others, and make choices. Mental health is important at every stage of life — from childhood and adolescence, continuing through adulthood. It plays an even more significant role after trauma. For example, it plays a huge role when you lose your child. I personally wanted and needed monitoring from my husband and my close family members in the event that I was acting out of character. I was well aware of how unpredictable and easily my moods were shifting.

The first step is being aware. Try and use someone else's common sense if yours isn't fully accessible. Get educated and be knowledgeable and then become mindful of your own mental health! Another step is being proactive. Mental health has now become more of a focus due to the statistics from sick children growing up to be sick adults. Though we have a long way to go, we are finally learning to do better. Delving into the correlations of unhealthy repeated patterns, childhood trauma, and how it manifests into our mentality are finally happening.

I've noticed a kinder, more empathetic approach to mental health, overall, from society. I've noticed more discussions period. We are now being more open about and talking about it. People seem more willing to self-reflect and to check their mental notes and status now. Be more mindful of the mind! That is really important. Maybe it's because you've had a family member, like me, who was constantly judged. Or maybe people just want better healthy relationships all around. Either way is good as long as we acknowledge that mental maintenance is key.

When I suffered from Candida in 2010, the infection was a major participant in my depression, especially when exasperated. In that, I urge you to test yourselves. After detoxing, I wondered just how I was functioning before. In retrospect, I was only minimally focusing. I was far from my best self. I was so grateful to take advantage of all my years of health education and use it on myself. Thankfully, my husband and I own four juice bars, which was completely inspired by our initial lifestyle change in 2009. We had been in the health food industry for almost a decade now. So, clearly, I know the effects of clean eating and juicing. That knowledge helped me fight the Candida! Hippocrates said, "Let thy food be thy medicine and medicine be thy food." The correlations between the body and the mind are astounding.

Everything is connected. Believe me! All you have to do is pay attention. God is your medical doctor and food is your prescription. Since we are what we eat, our mental capacity has the power to either induce problems or heal the body. This isn't me figuratively chit-chatting. I really care. My husband and I really care and wish happy and healthy lives for everyone. I don't know why the simplest things are the most difficult to attain and comprehend for us humans. You can control just about everything that goes on with your body on your own. So, when it comes to mental health, you can help yourself to a degree — a large degree!

My advice is to take the self-help plunge first before anything. Read and research. Most depression, hyperactivity, restlessness, and other issues are directly connected to your diet. If you already have a predisposition, inherited some kind of trait, and then your diet is poor, well, you do the math! This is a fact. Mental health should be a mandated subject in school and linked to how we care for our bodies, inside and out. It should be open for discussion at all times.

These two things are vital to a healthy mind: Positive eating and positive thinking. Society tells you to eat a good breakfast in the morning before school because it's the first fuel that you consume. Hence, it adds to your level of energy. A good healthy breakfast stimulates the mind, triggering productive thoughts while keeping the metabolism consistent.

The artificial blue drink, the beer, the Nathan's franks, the weed, plus missing home, wasn't giving Tai any bit of clarity. It was actually doing the complete opposite. It gave her anxiety and hypersensitivity that she wasn't even aware of — just the potential time for a bad day. I will share what I know and what I did to help keep her healthy up until that point. And, that's basically love, a good diet, exercise, arts of all kinds, and nature! These components made for a happy and healthy Tai and can make for a happy and healthy life for you too. With this, she was able to focus on the positives in life and not neglect her feelings. She was able to go on social media and casually see things that irritated her with little to no reactions and less of an impulsive reaction. I was able to see how my little experiment had worked. She was my test tube. Seeing the results from the diet (her new one) along with my mommy instincts, I knew that Tai was mentally off while in Florida.

My husband always said, "Never make any decisions or conduct convos while you are emotional or angered." We live by this! Typically, you're operating from an impulsive state. Most often, a non-sensible state — which is likely a temporary emotion. Those initial feelings will subside, which is why I know, as Tai's mother, that her passing was from her own impulsivity!

If you keep telling yourself repetitive, negative, and shameful thoughts, they fester and multiply, leaving you consumed and feeling trapped. You become trapped in your own thoughts from the direction of your own voice. It begins to make you feel as though the situation you're in is a reality, when in fact, you're overthinking, overemotional, and, sometimes, you're just over-exaggerating! This is not true in all cases, but it definitely is true in some. Learning to control and quiet the mind is so important. Stop listening, just shut it off. Play some music if you have to or if you like animals, go to a shelter — anything for a distraction. Understanding that my thoughts really shaped my mind was so key. Day by day by day, I would say, "Melodic thoughts over Adjua's thoughts."

If you're not strong or balanced enough, your career can be a hindrance as well. Everything that you regularly do in life should be evaluated and then reviewed so that you can see how it affects you, especially mentally. You need to assess how you started the job versus when you are years in. Regarding your health, you need to ask yourself if you have benefited or not. Your profession can interfere with your health. Asses your relationships. With kids, friends, perhaps your marriage has been affected. Negative feelings and unhappiness from work result in poor relationships overall too. Be mindful!

Tai never gave me the opportunity to know exactly what was going on. Maybe she couldn't even articulate her needs on her own just like I was unable to at times. I'll never know. Maybe she was ashamed of her thoughts. I don't know. Maybe I dropped the ball. Knowing how impulsive I was at that age, maybe I could have protected her more. Maybe I was too nonchalant. Maybe I was too naive. I'll never know. So, based on my perceptions and assumptions, I enforced a better diet, exercise, love, and support as my remedy for any of her ailments

Unfortunately, Afro-Americans already have a predisposition to suffering from depression. That's PTSS, and then infused with PTSD. PTSS is Post Traumatic Slave Syndrome, a study and theory on the lasting impact that generational slavery has had on the Afro-American community. PTSD is the most popular one. It is Post Traumatic Stress Disorder. We all have some element of PTSD, especially people of color. It's when you've experienced some sort of trauma (life-threatening), that triggers anxiety and you become emotional or have physical flashbacks of that experience. This is similar to what many, including myself, experience when pulled over by a police officer recollecting the lives we remember via hashtags due to police brutality. I believe that living in this world, news and politics alone can trigger PTSD.

Ultimately, this is your journey and your direction by your lead. Be deliberately in love with making the right choices for yourself and finding your own rhythm in life by finding you.

CHAPTER 15

Love & Live With No Regrets

1 Corinthians 13:4-8 embodies it all for me.

"4. Love is patient, love is kind. It does not envy, it does not boast, it is not proud. 5. It does not dishonor others, it is not self-seeking, it is not easily angered, it keeps no record of wrongs. 6. Love does not delight in evil but rejoices with the truth. 7. It always protects, always trusts, always hopes, always perseveres. 8. Love never fails. But where there are prophecies, they will cease; where there are tongues, they will be stilled; where there is knowledge, it will pass away." NIV®

Some of the most valuable and precious things in life are actually free or better yet, they cost nothing. Love and honesty are two of them. Being honest means that one has the integrity and the honor determined by an invisible resume. It is something that you either experience or hear by word of mouth. This resume reveals one's previous history and consistency. In other words, people know their track record in regard to how they've responded to situations — which is typically based on their ethics, morals, values, and principles that they live by. When a person is vigilant at being noble, I consider them a person of good integrity, which is essentially an honest person. Love is this enormous, unexplainable feeling, that is narrowed down to four seemingly inadequate letters to me. Ironically, people die, and countries have been at war over love — exhibiting just how powerful it is! The feeling that can offer is life changing. It is the most powerful energy humans can exchange.

Love is everything. It is the most powerful thing that exists. Love is lifting others via energy. Loves is also life's only vital energy. It is the most powerful energy we humans can exchange.

Love is greater than a feeling, although it is a feeling too. It makes you smile. It makes you curious. Love can trick and deceive you. Love will get its claws into you and grip your life, leaving you raw, open, and vulnerable. I had absolutely no regrets when my daughter passed. If I could go back, I doubt that I would have done anything differently because I loved her unconditionally and was brutally honest with my flaws regarding parenting. We worked out any issues that we had several years prior. The hormones were leveled up, Tai wasn't an adolescent anymore and I had to accommodate. She and I were truly at a fun stage in our lives. We were really living in love. She was a woman, a mature one now, and I was just honored to hang out with her. We passed the mommy and daughter stage; we were at the stage of respecting each other as adults — borderline girlfriends. Yet and still, Tai was very mindful of boundaries. Maybe I do have a regret. I regret getting super close to her because I'm having serious withdrawals. But, then again, if we weren't so close, I might not be able to connect with her as I do now. I live my life on a double-edged sword. I lived and still live like it's my last day! I close out the day with only positive interactions. I did feel overwhelmed at times with Tai. She really dominated all my time. I actually allowed her to because I felt like it would be over soon (her spending so much time with me — not actual death). I would spend as much time with her as possible — allowing tons and tons of memories to have been made. Because of this, I am so thankful to God — that was His doing. Things could have always gone another way.

Generationally, we all carry a load of laundry (emotional baggage) with us. We are trying to beat the odds as a parent by not repeating certain patterns and behaviors that were introduced to us as a child. Tai was happy and loved her family. Everyone knew that! And, we did the best we could with what God gave us. I commend any man who steps up for another man's child. Hats off to you! I tried to cover all angles when it came to Tai. I believe she knew that, which is why I always kept the love first! And, it has always been reciprocated from my kids.

The feeling that love gives you is organic and unstoppable. Love is not abusive.

Love is an uncontrollable, jovial, happy; a warm feeling. However, love has confused me at times. I have allowed love to conjure negative thoughts in myself that I never knew were possible. Mainly, it was because my idea was distorted. I got most of my notions of what love or what being loved was from television. If you mix that in with my childhood beliefs of what love was, I was confused. Then, developed upon those notions.

Clearly, I was operating from someone else's state of mind. Never once did I really focus on what I wanted my idea of love to be. I just loved the way that I perceived it. It was okay to break any cycles and go after what I wanted by designing my idea of what love was.

Through time, experiences, and ultimately being married, I've now learned about the authenticity and freedom of love. In doing so, I'm giving back to me, my core self, and what resonates in me. It's all love because now that I've learned, moving forward, I've taught people how to treat me. It's a win-win for everyone; everyone is happy.

Love is primarily what connects us together and attracts us to each other whether one is aware or not. You have that genuine feeling; we all have it — whether you want to act on it or not. It is there. It exists. It is inside of you. You can't be a bystander when someone gets hurt and say, "Oh how nice!" It is not a natural response. Your desire to inquire and help someone is an act of love. Empathy is love. You can't even walk by a pretty flower, bird, or woman for that matter, without acknowledging the beauty. Yeah, you may not notice it right away! But, when you do, you admire it.

You're actually admiring God, which is love.

When I admire a beautiful painting that someone made, I am most likely in awe of their talent. Of course, I'm acknowledging their craft and art, but I'm also acknowledging his God given talents and abilities. I am not just admiring the product. I am admiring the mind behind the project. It goes much deeper than just the surface. God created the individual's talent. In that case, God is the original painter. He chooses you and gives you your job! He created us all with our own magic. We just have to unleash it. I'm not religious, but I definitely reap the benefits of prayer. I pray all the time and I believe in God, the source, the Creator!

It doesn't make you a coward or a pushover to show love. Some people have that image, but that isn't the truth. Love is truth. It actually exudes strength and shows how connected to the universe you are. It's attractive and beautiful. Yes, love is attractive. The more you love, the more love you'll receive. You will! I've learned it and I live it!

I used to have a very hard time with forgiveness. I had a problem with forgiveness in all of its angles — inside and out, upside and down. I had a real big problem with that word. But not understanding and exercising forgiveness was making me ill and it was making me depressed. I am thankful to my husband for the supportive pep talks. Once I learned or at least got on the road to learning forgiveness, a new world opened up. And, the icing on the cake, (the best part of it all), is that you have now released the waste, allowing the universe to do its job — ushering in some karma via white-glove service. I seriously had no faith in karma. I wasn't aware of her endless capabilities. When I comprehended the notion of forgiveness, then forgave, and saw karma come to fruition, it meant that I could walk away feeling satisfied. Forgiveness is a combination of things. Forgiveness is freeing yourself, trusting in God, and not blocking any blessings from coming your way — loving yourself.

True love is consistent because it is impossible to stop — whether it is a platonic or romantic relationship, it is an undeniable feeling. Even if consistent inconsistency is your thing, it can still be considered love. It's not what you do. It's how you do it. In other words, you can be faulty in your delivery and capability of showing love, but it doesn't necessarily always mean you love anyone less. Hence, me accepting my husband's approach to romance. It is a bit convoluted at times. However, I know that I'm loved. He means well, which equates to sweet intentions that symbolize love.

Tai's love was true love!

It was real love. Tai is love! Tai's heart was so big that she waddled when she walked. She went above and beyond to show you how much she cared about you. Leaving little notes here and there or letting you know that you were thought of by picking up something for you on her travels. She wouldn't stop until she made you feel loved and you were left with a tremendously big, toothy smile — something comparable to hers.

I believe that she used love as her angle. Even at twenty, she still drew hearts on everything. I am so blessed to have had Tai and to have been a part of her human life and to be her mother. Gratefully, her spirit thrives heavily in my life. I feel her everywhere. All she did was love and she wanted to be loved, which was definitely a Capricorn trait. She exuded love. Anyone who had a solid connection with her can attest to that, even some acquaintances as well! I miss being wrapped up in her love. And on the days when I miss it the most, I read a text of hers, "Can we cuddle tonight?"

And, that's what love does. It wraps you in its arms no matter the trauma you've faced. Love tucks you in at night and reminds you there is a glorious morning ahead.

Afterword

One day, I had the most perfect family with all the trimmings — well-mannered, articulate minors embarking on adulthood. The next day, I'm trying to wrap my head around flying to Florida to identify the body of my first-born. My Tai. Pacifying sentiments and gestures are appreciated. However, they ultimately won't stop the embers in my heart that still burn for her. When the closest human to you crosses over, you're left perplexed to say the least — wondering if lives are just to be sacrificed for some greater goal. You're also left questioning God about his frivolous moves in this strategic game of life.

I never wanted to be a survivor. I always thought that they were weak, poverty-stricken, and broken individuals. I used to think that the image of a survivor was either a recuperated fetal alcohol baby that had been born in the ICU or an amputated veteran trying to maintain a copacetic life. Being a gullible young empath, I even believed the propaganda smear regarding third world countries and how horrible their living conditions were — rendering deep concerns and sorrow in me as a kid and believing that mostly everyone lived in destitution.

Empathy, compassion, and support - all sentiments of love - come naturally from this tender heart. Therefore, I see those people as indestructible souls — the ones plastered all over the news. They are born survivors in my eyes.

However, now that I am the walking definition of a survivor and am more accustomed to our makeup, I now feel that it's quite the contrary. Survivors are some of the strongest people I know. We thrive through it all. It's like a sad badge of honor that indicates an invisible strength. And because of it, I have now redirected some of the empathy that I had for others to myself. Tai's life and death has given me insight, forcing me to delve into the ugliest, darkest pockets of my life, which is something that I will never regret. This book is ultimately the culmination of a major cleanse.

The hardest gifts to explain are the ones that are intangible. Hence, this explains the privilege of losing a child. Tai's crossover initially put me in a place of despair. It put me in such hopelessness that only God could help or understand. It forced me to have an intensely intimate relationship with him — a relationship that is expressed through love, compassion, and truth. Tai, perhaps your precocious soul was here for many specific purposes — like helping to encourage your family to unite and appreciate the present or giving us the opportunity to appreciate the ability to touch, to hug, and to love in the physical. This is something that we humans take for granted. Only time will tell.

I didn't profess to be a doctor or anyone who had all the answers, not one time throughout my testimony. I'm sharing my truth, my weaknesses, and what has made me stronger. I am the one who lived and experienced my life firsthand. Therefore, I can speak on what works for me, my survival skills, and my family's survival skills. I've learned and have come to understand that my first line of defense is my health and with that strength alone, I can be more effective. With this power, I can combat everyday life by being woke from within.

For me, honoring my body in this way allows my mind to think clearly. If I'm human and have an off day with muddled thoughts, then guess what? I'm only human. We must learn to be more understanding and sensitive with ourselves. We need to learn as much as we can about ourselves. We all need to learn what makes us tick and the ins and outs of ourselves! Then, you will have more patience and tolerance — ultimately understanding a leopard cannot change his spots.

In turn, you will nurture your own individuality and have less judgement and concern of what other people think. It's easy to point fingers while I try to put the pieces of my life's puzzle together as you sit in your glass house. You would literally need an anointed resume, with God's signature on it for me to sincerely value your opinion. As of now, the only spirit, human, or entity close to that description is the medium. I needed to bring her in so that I could explain the connections because in life, everything connects. Synchronization is a current theme in my life and when I finally grasped the whole concept, life changed for me. I viewed everything differently, everything became a piece of my puzzle from either my past or where I'm presently going. While there are definitely obvious synchronizations that I consider, I believe that God has the ultimate say. As a mother, I stand firm in the belief that I did my best. I was working with the best intelligence that I had, and I never stopped loving her unconditionally. I will always love her —unconditionally. Tai has been my greatest gift! My greatest love, Tai, the one who teaches me to thrive.

I love you Tai.
I love you all.
Thank you for reading! Viva Para Siempre Tai!

"To whom much is given, much is required." –
One of life's greatest lessons

Notes

Tai...My best friend. My mentor. My partner in crime, bane, and kryptonite. Tai. She's always been there for me mentally and spiritually in the past, present, and in the future. With guidance ranging from how to coordinate the colors in my outfits, or how to talk to girls, to making good and bad decisions growing up. We showed each other what true loyalty and trust meant. She showed me what honor, pride, and demanding respect looked like. She is the only person, to this day, with whom I have shared true, uncut, unfiltered joy and laughter with, as well as a sacred bond with—secrets that will never be spoken. Without her, I may have never pushed and aspired to make music. Without her, I probably wouldn't have many friends or a sense of humor. It would be easy to admit, "I wouldn't be me without her." But, it's not easy to admit. I question my ability to grow and to stay properly aligned on my path without her. So, instead of looking back, I look forward. I take the gems, the blessings and the teachings, and let her live through me. She can share my love and all of my light. Sharing is caring. Right?

Sincerely, Jeff (Noah)

PS. I have doggy treats.

To the parents of Tai, I'm really sorry for the loss of your daughter. It's so tragic to lose a loved one at such an early age. I can't imagine the pain that your family is going through. Please know that you're in my thoughts and prayers. I'm truly humbled to know that Tai was such a big fan. I am forever grateful that she loved my music and believed in me. Rest easy Tai on that island in the sky.

Humbly submitted,
Fetty Wap

Acknowledgements

God - because without him nothing is possible. My human shell for not breaking down. My spirit guides for they keep me going. I must thank my husband for his wisdom, patience, will, and his love. My perpetual teachers, Noah and Tai, thank you for loving me unconditionally and being my greatest gifts. Thank you mom and dad for hosting my free soul and not putting me away for my unorthodox spirit. Melinda (stepmom), thank you for putting up with me and loving my dad unconditionally. I want to thank my mother-in-law for always being a model of dignity and strength. I would like to thank Alison for still loving Tai and being a daughter to me. Amina, you are a loyal force to be reckoned with. I appreciate you for always standing with me, my sister. Joyce you are a mother/sister/aunt and most importantly a great friend. Thank you for filling in the gaps and keeping me spiritually grounded. Andy, I cannot thank you enough for all you've done for me. You're like an Italian knight for my family. Your light is so bright and I'm so grateful to have been touched by it for over twenty years. My sisters, Martha and Holly, thank you for your love and support and for keeping my family constantly in your prayers since '09. Jamal Ibrahim and Ravon Jones thank you guys for not only being amazing brothers to my husband but for always taking time out for my kids throughout the years, even when you've had your own - thanks bros. Margarite Camaj you are a beautiful talented wizard. I thank you for not knowing me from Adam and diligently and genuinely delivering for me. My sister-in-law Tamisha and friend Tiffany thank you for taking Tai to endless birthday parties and park runs, she and I thoroughly appreciated it. Kristi thanks for loving Tai and being a liaison with and her music. I appreciate and thank you for supporting my family. A special shout out to Angela Yee and Tasha Hilton, you guys inspired this entire project, I humbly thank you. Thank you to the team at Tasha Hilton Publishing Company, Chelcee Johns, Pauleanna Reid and everyone at Writers Blok. Brielle, thank you for being an awesome friend to Tai and her family. Farmacy For Life family, Juices For Life family, Dr. Sebi, Dr. Theresra, Dr. Oz, Own Network *Super Soul Sunday*, Ritz Carlton family (White Plains), Lyn Leclaire (medium), Christian Boonlong (graphic designer), and James Watson. I am beyond grateful and want to sincerely thank you all for being an integral part of this process. I want to thank every person who was a part of Tai's life. Again, thank you from my whole heart and I love you!

CPSIA information can be obtained
at www.ICGtesting.com
Printed in the USA
BVHW032131190220
572875BV00001B/16